SINGLE THAT

*Dispelling The Top 10 Myths Of
The Single Woman*

Acamea Deadwiler

Dedicated to my niece India, and every young girl who will one day be a woman deserving of empowered existence.

Contents

SINGLE.

I wrote two beginnings for this book—one where I was in a happy, committed relationship and the other being single. I've been in both situations during the course of its completion, but I won't say which one I am currently in because I believe that it influences the way opinions on this subject matter are received. If I'm single, what I have to say will be immediately dismissed by some as coming from a place of bitterness. If I'm in a relationship, my thoughts may come across as condescending or uninformed. Like "oh you've found someone so now you know it all." This is a lose-lose situation.

So, I won't say. Instead, I hope that my words will be received as what they are, sincere. These words and ideas are coming from someone who believes deeply in the power and wonder of love. Yet, I've been notoriously known as a single woman for most of my adult life. Despite being referred to by some as attractive, funny, engaging, and an overall "catch" (thank you), I've journeyed most of my path alone.

I will tell you that I haven't been in a long-term, serious, committed romantic relationship since I was about nineteen years old. I'm thirty-six as I begin writing this. Yikes. The years that have passed really just hit me for the first time. Though I have lived this life eyes-wide-open, I never noticed it before. Maybe seeing the numbers in print and being forced to calculate the interval is what did it. It's never been something I've really thought about and doesn't feel that long ago. But almost twenty years have gone by since spending two summers and every other season with my first and only love.

Wow.

We met while working together at Burger King. Still in high school, it was both our first jobs. He wasn't someone I'd normally connect with. We had very different backgrounds. Raised by a family of devout Christians who sheltered me from anything deemed unholy, I was extremely naïve compared to the street-savvy, mature way of thinking he'd been afforded by a more lenient upbringing. He was a bad boy who made himself good, for me.

I mean, I really loved him. We were together and talked all the time. Whether out, at home, or on the phone, I never grew tired of him the way that I did others. He was my best friend, biggest supporter, and greatest source of inspiration. I was different with him, softer. No topic of discussion was off-limits or uncomfortable for us. We were psychologically naked in front of one another. It was the pure expression of fondness that you hope to achieve with someone.

I loved him so much that when wrongfully accused by a friend of his of being seen with another guy, I broke down in tears trying to convince him that it wasn't true. He told me he needed time to think, and

I was distraught, hoping with everything within me that he didn't decide to end our relationship. I don't know if I was more upset at the idea of losing him, at the thought of him feeling that I'd betrayed him, or because it would all be the result of a false claim. The point is that I cared more about the outcome than I had cared about anything in a long time. Thankfully, my love came to his senses and we continued writing our story.

We grew apart as adulthood approached. Yet, despite our differences, clearly no one has been able to take his place. Not in nearly TWENTY YEARS! Nonetheless, I've never looked back. I've always felt certain that our time together had run its course. Now I'm at the tail end of my thirties with no children, and having never been married, not even close.

I've had some fun, dated people exclusively, and been in relationships here and there, but none of substance. For years I would go, unattached and uninvolved. Sometimes I think I may have spent the best years of my life this way, and I wonder if they were wasted. Then again, you know that saying about how youth is wasted on the young? So, maybe not. Maybe the beauty of love and relationships is wasted on the ill-prepared.

Regardless of what my relationship status will be when I finish this book or when you read it, this viewpoint is coming from someone who's been where I'm about to take you. I think I've paid enough dues for a lifetime of single woman expertise. I've likely forgotten more than most others have learned on the topic.

Overall, I never had an issue with being single, though I may have had my days and my nights where I desired for it to not be so. Others seemed to be more concerned with my singledom than I ever was. Actually, they seem overly concerned with single people in general. I've seen so many unprovoked social media posts and heard so much bad advice directed at those who are single, when no one asked for it.

I don't get why anyone cares so much. When I'm single, or even when I'm not, I don't obsess over other people's relationships. I don't care what they're doing or feel compelled to tell them how to do it better. This is especially true with people I don't actually know. I don't sit up and try to dissect anyone's marriage from afar and attack aspects that may make it appear as though the union is not fruitful. I'm too concerned with maintaining my own happiness to worry myself with someone else's.

Yet, people, usually those who are one half of a married couple, will write Facebook dissertations aimed at individuals who are single. They'll tell you why you're in what they deem to be a predicament, and implore fellow married or involved followers not to listen to anything you have to say. In a sense, they look down on those who are single as though nothing of value can be offered from this position. Never mind their own crumbling, inauthentic relationships. This isn't always the case, but there are absolutely those who climb up on a relationship high horse even if theirs is unhealthy. As though being with someone in and of itself is better than being alone.

I have nothing against commitment and relationships. I believe that marriage can be a formidable source of joy, love, and support. It can be an amazing experience that adds positive elements to our lives. I also respect being single and don't categorize either status above the other. I know that there is joy to be found in being unattached as well. There is peace and precious, needed time to ourselves.

So when I witness bashing or arrogance as it relates to being single, I don't get it. It has confused and sometimes annoyed me for a few different reasons; mainly the insinuation that there is something inherently wrong with the circumstance.

For those people who are reading this and are in romantic relationships, I beg of you, don't treat your single friends like a problem that needs to be solved. Do not speak of them as "single" as though that is who they are. Seems so silly to me, using one's relationship status as a defining quality. I recognize that often many of you may actually mean well, and you simply want your friends and loved ones to be happy. However, therein lies the problem, the assumption that being single is so horrible that they couldn't possibly be happy as-is. But I get it when coming from those with the best of intentions, your friend is awesome and you want someone else to see and cherish his or her awesomeness.

I'll focus mainly on single women because of the double standard in perception that we all know exists regarding the sexes. Please, I don't care to visit pretend-land and debate this one. If you haven't accepted by now that women are viewed differently and held to more rigid societal standards than men in this department, you probably won't like what's coming next.

There are no absolutes. When referencing men, women, friends, etc., it doesn't mean *all* men, women, and friends. But common misconceptions become such because they're, well, common.

Even the best experiences become better when shared. I don't underestimate the impact of having someone with whom to embark on life's journey. I *love* love, and believe in it as well. I have seen it in all of its genuine, selfless magnificence. So I know it exists. The issue comes when its value is overstated, to the point where not having said person is viewed as a circumstance that is "less than" and a life unfulfilled.

Such a distorted perception leads friends to focus on this sole aspect of your life. As a result, they try to pimp or whore you out every chance they get (figuratively, of course, hopefully). There is constant badgering about why you're single and what happened to that one guy you were dating for five minutes, as well as funny looks when you tell them you're not interested in someone. Almost as though you don't have the luxury of not being interested at a certain point. It consumes interactions and comes up in some form, somehow, someway at every social gathering.

It's the scarlet letter "S" on your chest, and it doesn't stand for Superwoman in their eyes, though that would be more fitting. They gawk at you in amazement. Overly intrigued, they want to delve into your existence and find out how you are making your way through the world, carrying on as though you, alone, are enough.

Perhaps in reality it's not as bad as it may seem. The replay of situations in our minds is usually worse than it was in real-time. It's just that the process of dating, of waiting, of disappointment, and starting over again can be draining enough all on its own, without this added element of having to constantly discuss, defend, and downplay it all. Such behavior, unwarranted, can imply a great deal regarding what you think about a person, even if not overtly.

It implies that you don't think the single woman can just go out and have a good time without being on the prowl for a man; that she should be on the prowl for a man; that she needs a man; and that she wants every man she sees or compliments. "He's married" is not a necessary response to the simply stated, "He's handsome."

Behaving this way with your single friend subtly attaches many labels to her, none of which are flattering.

Single.

THAT DOES NOT MEAN DESPERATE

I recognize that one can only comprehend a situation from personal level of understanding. Thus, a woman who is always on the prowl for a partner when single will attach this objective to the status. When she has friends who are single, she may assume they are hunting for a man, as this is the way she behaves in similar situations.

I don't believe there is a right or wrong way to approach dating. So, I'm attaching no negative inferences to being on the prowl for a man. If having a man is something that a woman considers important and urgent enough to engage in aggressive pursuit, that's her prerogative! I sometimes wish I were as vocal and vulnerable in this area as women who take the lead and go after who they want. When someone else shoves this method down my throat, however, it never feels empowering. Partly because they don't seem to care about my lack of consent, and partly because it's an inaccurate implication related to my state of mind.

True in most cases is that the way a person behaves in general has little to do with anyone else. We treat people a certain way, make decisions about others, and act according to our own set of beliefs. Our view of the world is cultivated mostly by individual experience. What is displayed externally comes from within.

I am trying to look at this from both sides and consider viable, non-offensive explanations for such preposterous assumptions. I am trying to offer the benefit of the doubt, and understand why it is often rare that a single woman can go anywhere with friends without the mention and analysis of men in the room on her behalf.

"He's an attorney. What do you mean you're not interested?"

Questions like this have been repeatedly asked of me. Being frank, this exact question, with various alternate job titles inserted, has been repeatedly asked of me. Fellow ladies just could not believe that I would have no interest in pursuing an attorney. I literally got the "What the hell is wrong with you" face in response.

In this particular situation, I simply didn't find the guy attractive. Physical appearance isn't the most important factor in a potential mate, but it is important. Oftentimes I think we underrate this aspect in attempts to not appear shallow. I do believe that attraction can increase once you get to know a person and are drawn to particular attributes. So this was not a deal-breaker, but there being no initial lure meant there was no initial curiosity on my part. I would not have been opposed to meeting him and seeing what happened, but I wasn't going to jump on the opportunity based on knowing nothing except what he did for a living.

You have to understand the way I view and approach relationships. I'm more impressed by who someone is as a person than what he or she does or has accomplished. I also do alright for myself financially. So, I can't be swayed by the idea of being taken care of. I'm not going to just pounce on a guy because he's an attorney or a doctor or in any other prominent, lucrative profession. This alone doesn't automatically constitute an ideal mate, in my opinion. Stability and ambition are heavily weighted in my book of desires, but less tangible qualities such as integrity and discipline matter more.

Perhaps the attorney had these qualities and excelled in matters of character as well. I wouldn't know without learning more about him. Like I said, I was open to meeting him. I'm open to being introduced to just about anyone. I didn't feel compelled to do so just because he appeared successful. I don't fall over myself to get to anyone, especially not based on elements without substance.

The other side to the shock of my being unimpressed by possible partner candidates at an event is the "sorry, there're no potentials here" unprompted apology when there are none. Even if you make no comments or inquiries remotely related to whether there are eligible bachelors in attendance, some feel the need to express remorse for the lack of a feasible dating pool. It's as though the revelation is a letdown. But it doesn't stop there, of course not.

If you're in a group setting, next comes the announcements of how everyone needs to search for someone to pair with you. After all, in case anyone didn't know, YOU'RE SINGLE. If someone in the circle speaks to or references knowing a guy, it's "hook him up with my friend." Never mind that you haven't so much as batted an eye or even seem to care, this is of the utmost importance, apparently.

No matter how many times you say, "I'm fine," some in your circle just ignore it and are even bewildered. There's no comprehensible way that you can be fine in their opinion. And don't show up to any occasion dressed well—it will be viewed as you're trying to seduce everyone.

This is even more exhausting than it sounds.

Maybe some single women enjoy incessant matchmaking efforts. Perhaps some actually *are* always scouring the room for men and want all-hands-on-deck in support of this cause. As I said, I'm not mad at it. Do your thing. I can only speak for myself and women like me who feel differently.

Is it really so inconceivable that a single woman can actually have a great time with her girlfriends, out at a concert, having a drink, dinner, or otherwise? Is it that far-fetched to believe a woman can enjoy things she does alone? Contrary to often-popular opinion, these things are possible. Some women can genuinely enjoy the company, the outing, and themselves with no ulterior motives or desires.

People assume being unattached has to be eating you up inside; that it consumes your every thought. True, if you are single and looking, meeting someone new is always nice. But I view it as an added bonus when it happens, not a requirement for deeming the outing a success. I also find it fascinating that others can be more concerned about the situation than the person whom it affects. The need to constantly verbalize the concern, to me, is all the more peculiar. Especially if the person always seems happy and unbothered. That is what leads me to question the motive, which can be either sincere or self-serving.

While some just truly want to help, and think that's what they're doing. Others seek to flex their superiority complex revolving around relationship status. Reminding everyone and making a big deal about you being single also lets it be known that they're not. They have someone. The men in attendance are not of their concern. This is a fact of which they are proud, borderline boastful. These fellows are of concern for the single woman, however, at least in their opinion.

Then there are the guys who you meet while single, especially if you have no children and are no longer in your twenties. I had a younger guy ask me if I was scared during our first conversation. Verbatim, his text message read, (in response to my willingness to wait rather than have kids with someone just to have them):

> "Yeah, I definitely understand that but soon in about four years you will be 40. You're not scared? Or paranoid about that?" To which I replied, "What is there to be scared of?"

This assumption that a woman cannot live a full life without kids or marriage is both demeaning and saddening. It's so much bigger than me and rooted in deep-seated societal issues that I don't know where to begin in an attempt to even address the notion. Our history of established gender roles is finally starting to be unraveled a bit, but still exists in the minds of many.

I do want kids someday, and even to possibly be a wife. However, I want a lot of things that I will not consider the be-all and end-all regarding the quality of my existence. I want to travel (possibly even more than I want children!), learn to play an instrument, publish a book of poetry, own a successful business, and maybe land a movie role. For the record I dream big, often without rhyme or reason.

Yet here comes a guy, claiming to like me, who cares only about one aspect of my abilities. One that was given to me without my having to do anything to earn it. I was born capable of bearing children. There are so many other things I've worked to achieve and become. Adding insult to injury, he basically insinuates that there is an expiration date on being selective and patient, while barely even being able to fathom a woman actually comfortable with her single status at a certain "age."

The flip side of this is that men will assume that if single and childless after age thirty, you'll pressure them to have children because *your* time is running out. They see your biological clock ticking, and you can only press snooze a couple of times. Yet, "I need to hurry up and have kids" is honestly a thought that has never entered my mind. If it happens, wonderful. If it doesn't, I'll still live a full life with the understanding that being a mother is not a part of my journey. As difficult as it may be to believe, that's okay with me.

Girls are taught that they're supposed to bear and raise children. Many grow up believing that this is their reason for being, their duty. Life is deemed incomplete without this variable. Girls become women who feel pressure to get pregnant and struggle with feelings of inadequacy that have been projected onto them if they cannot.

The pressure is both self-inflicted and a result of outside influence. There is this sense of obligation to proving maternal worth. When a woman remains childless into her thirties, that's really all people want to hear about. It's just expected that you will or should be having children soon. If not, there will be questions. Man or woman, actually, people constantly ask when you're going to have kids. The ticks of that biological clock can grow deafening for some women.

All other achievements are overshadowed. Never mind the promotion you just got at work, the book you finally finished writing, your trip to Italy, or the beautiful home you purchased. Nothing will supersede everyone's preoccupation with the one thing they seem to care about most, you having a baby. The life-altering feat is treated as another item to cross off of a to-do list. Like, at a certain point, this is just next up. Extenuating circumstances be damned.

Worse, the concept of a woman simply deciding that she does not want any children is downright blasphemous to some people. They don't understand. How can you not want to do the thing you were designed to do? This perspective reveals how someone really views women. The choice wouldn't be so difficult to fathom for anyone who considers women to be much more than baby-making machines. Just because we *can* do something doesn't mean we must, or even that we should.

I never bought into that idea. Motherhood wasn't something to which I aspired. I have friends who fantasized about it all, eager to start families. In hindsight, I'm sure they'd agree they probably went a step further and romanticized several aspects. Like every other mental picture, it looks a lot easier and much more fun in your head. I wasn't against the notion. Just never had that "oooooh I can't wait to be a mom" urge. Though I think I'd be a great one.

I feel no pressure and am in no rush. Having children is not a factor in measuring my self-worth. It saddens me that for many of my peers, it is. We feel broken, as though we are somehow less of a woman if we can't get pregnant or carry a child to term. We continue to exist within the constraints of a box filled with markers for external validation.

For those who genuinely want children and are unable to conceive or carry them, I won't presume to understand how devastating this can be. I know someone who struggled with this situation. I know how hard she tried and how deeply wounding futile efforts became. The exhaustion and disappointment of being filled with joy once pregnant, then suffering a miscarriage is something I cannot even begin to grasp. But I can imagine. For these women, I must be sure to not diminish the effects of such circumstances or underestimate the weight of such a burden.

Many women desire children and a family and would do so even if outside influence did not exist. I feel compelled to drive home my respect for women to whom this is important and the decision to have kids in and of itself. Some women choose to adopt even if they face no barriers to childbirth. They just want to help, raise, and love a child.

I do believe in maternal instincts; and that women are somewhat conditioned, with all of our estrogen and other assorted hormones, to nurture and care. My main point here is that it doesn't mean it's unnatural not to want children or to be indifferent to the idea of having them. When the state of motherhood is not tied to your sense of purpose, you view it differently. For me, it is an option that I feel fortunate to have. But it remains only one option of many for the direction of my life. If I do not take advantage of this opportunity, I don't think I'll feel as though something is missing.

If I don't have kids I'll still be happy. I'll travel and learn of different cultures. I'll do things that bring me joy, and there are many. I'll discover even more pleasures and take advantage of the hours, days, and resources that I'll have to enjoy such things; not to mention the ability to just get up and go at a moment's notice.

I'm sure nothing compares to the feeling of bringing a life into the world, seeing a piece of yourself in a little human, watching him or her grow, and receiving his or her unconditional love. I have no doubt that it's an immensely rewarding experience. It's just not the only one that matters or is available.

If I don't have kids I'll love on my nieces and nephews, hard. I already do this, so the loving would simply continue without any loss of intensity. I'll support their dreams and make sure they never lack anything that is within my power to provide. All of the motherly instincts, nurturing, and adoration that I may have stored inside will be poured into them. I think that's a pretty worthy place for it to go.

I'll relish my abundant "me time." If I don't have kids, I'll know that I am not any less significant. I'll focus on my mental, physical, emotional, and spiritual well-being. My wants and needs will receive unrivaled attention as I work to grow into the very best, whole, and healthy version of myself.

If I don't have kids I will still be a woman who makes a difference and offers valuable contributions to the world. I will be a productive member of society and give much more than I take. I'll leave people better than I found them. I'll lead a fulfilled, inherently important life. I'll live, love, and laugh unapologetically out loud.

If I don't have kids, I'll lean on the strength of my belief that motherhood does not define a woman. It surely won't define me.

I may have days where I'll think back and wonder what my child may have been like. I'll also look back and wonder how different my life would have been had I chosen a different major in college or had a better understanding of finances, earlier. I don't reflect with regret necessarily, more with curiosity. A daydream of sorts. The weight of it all is the same to me. We make our choices and walk our paths.

Needless to say, the relationship with that guy never materialized into anything meaningful. This story was only a small piece of our limited conversations. He went on to state how a woman cannot be happy for too long without a significant other, scoff after being told I was lying in bed and my answer to his question of whether I was alone was "yes," exclaim that I would be fifty saying the same things I'm saying now, and accusing me of looking for the "perfect man" when we had never even met or discussed what I wanted in a significant other.

When I pointed this out, that he was making assumptions based solely on the fact that I was single in my thirties, and someone who he found attractive, he disagreed. But it was clear. This was our first conversation. We'd never discussed anything about me, my past relationships, qualities that appeal to me, or anything to that effect. To him, I was the stereotypical single woman who was strong-willed to a fault. He didn't need to know me because he felt he knew the type that he prematurely deemed me to be.

There's a clichéd misconception that men are single because they choose to be, but women are single because they *have* to be. Men don't get nearly the same stigma or reaction as women in the exact situation. A single man is considered to be living his life and having fun being free.

I recently came across a familiar face on a dating app. This guy and I had never met, but I was using the app off and on for maybe a couple of years. We seemed to always "match" with each other but never actually get together in person. That's the thing with dating apps and the endless fish in the sea. You match with so many people that there's no way you'll ever take the encounter off-app with most of them.

Anyway, this guy and I matched again. After which he proceeds to send me a message saying something along the lines of, "Dang! You're STILL on here? You must be too picky!" I immediately thought, *But you're here too*! The fact that he considered it odd that I was still on the app, clearly not thinking that it's the same as him still being on the app, speaks volumes.

Maybe I should be flattered by men having such a hard time accepting my being single that they have to come up with blame-riddled reasons. I guess I could take it as some sort of compliment. The lens that I filter such reactions through may be jaded. In cases such as this though, it's the negative undertone that makes it difficult for me to see it this way.

In both instances I've mentioned, the guys decided there was some problem with my outlook or process that was keeping me single. I'm not above looking at myself and any areas where I can improve. Personal development is my jam. It's again the assumptions that rub me the wrong way. Saying, "Wow, you're so amazing that I can't believe you're single" is quite different from analyzing my status from the standpoint of what I'm doing wrong, especially with severely limited information.

Then there is the successful man who offers some type of service or does work that involves interacting with the public. He's what you would call an ideal potential partner. He has his life together, seems like a good person, and is attractive. This guy often tends to presume that a single woman who engages in conversation or requests his services is trying to get close to him. It can go two ways; if single and interested, the guy will read more into the situation than is there and possibly cross that professional line. If uninterested or involved, he'll feel inclined to make you aware unprovoked, and not in a casual *here's a picture of my family* type of way either. This is a common gripe I've heard, as well as experienced myself on occasion.

I can respect shutting down any flirting before it gets out of hand if in a relationship or not even allowing the door to be opened. I'm sure it happens. Maybe even frequently. But at least wait until the woman gives some indication that this is the case and says or does something questionable. Don't just assume she wants you because she's single. Please. Get over yourself. Maybe she just thinks you're cool. Maybe she's just being nice. Or perhaps she actually needs the professional services.

(Insert deep sigh)

Much of this goes back to the gender roles in our society that I mentioned earlier. Women are trained, whether inadvertently or not, to aspire to marriage. However, men aren't taught the same. Yet, they know that this is what women are taught. So there is this underlying sense among them that women are trying to tie them down and are after them on some level. This creates even bigger issues than just thinking a single woman is a desperate barracuda. It results in problems such as a dating disconnect.

The best way I can describe dating between men and women is two trains moving in opposite directions that somehow end up in a head-on collision.

In essence, we're usually not on the same track or traveling similar journeys. Yet, we find our way to each other and someone detours off of his or her path in favor of the other's. But because it was never actually the desired route, they don't always stay there.

This is compounded by the climate of our social circles. Boys who become men are high-fived for having sex with women, especially a woman who is highly sought after. It's treated as some kind of feat that has been accomplished. He is the envy of all men. On the other side, women are degraded if thought to have slept with too many guys. (Whatever ambiguous number that is.)

Men are put on a pedestal. Girls grow into women believing that to have a man is a privilege. We're taught how to get a man, keep a man, and treat a man. Rarely is anyone relaying the same message to them as it pertains to us. Girls become competitors, for the attention of men—for the great honor of having a man find them sexually desirable.

The biggest problem with such polarizing values and perceptions of romantic relationships between the sexes is that we're expecting these men to love us. These same men, who have spent their lives in an environment that encourages sleeping with as many women as they can and having as much fun as possible are expected to offer something more meaningful. This leaves women, the ones who've aspired to marriage and family and done their best to become suitable "wife material," with intentions that are rarely reciprocated.

The result is women pursuing relationships with men who are simply pursuing women and labeled desperate because of it. But that's a conversation for another book.

Single.

THAT DOES NOT MEAN LONELY

I am well aware that there are women (and men) who do not enjoy being by themselves. Some are highly uncomfortable, bored, and even sad when alone. So they keep a room full of people. They have roommates, not for help with living expenses, but because they like the company. Being able to divvy up the rent and other bills is merely an added incentive.

There's nothing wrong with enjoying companionship. Some of us are more social than others. There are introverts and extroverts and those teetering somewhere in the middle. To some, quiet is peaceful, to others it's maddening. Being a people person isn't a limitation. To be consistently surrounded by love, attention, and support is quite healthy. It's probably a lot of fun, too.

However, you can't really know yourself unless you spend time with yourself, independent of the needs and influence of others. We've all gone somewhere or done something that didn't really interest us because it's what someone else wanted. That's fine in moderation. But when that's our life—when just about every second of every day involves another person, there is an imbalance that can quickly develop into one that is self-harming.

Naturally, we become the version of ourselves that fits best with those in our circle. Many of us don't remember who we were before parents, friends, and society made us someone else. In spending time alone, we get to hear our thoughts without all of the outside noise. We learn our authentic likes and dislikes, what we need, and who we are. If we avoid spending time alone because doing so makes us unhappy, I believe that *is* an issue.

I'm sure there are many who can attest to the fact that you can be in a room full of people and still feel lonely. Warm bodies don't automatically fill voids. You can sleep next to a significant other every night and still feel lonely. Married couples feel lonely. This state of being is not reserved for those who are single. Yet, if you are a woman and single, it's a frequent assumption.

Women have more things to do than serve men. Surprise! I know that may be hard for some to believe. But many of us actually have dreams and goals that occupy our time and leave little opportunity to feel lonely. I've had my moments, but I was never coming home and crying into my pillow every night, overcome with the sadness of isolation. I was coming home and writing, researching, doing homework for school, watching my favorite shows, reading, drinking wine, and relaxing. Most of the time, I would sincerely enjoy that space to myself where I could have solace and silence if that was what I desired.

In full disclosure, the Myers-Briggs personality test confirms what I've always known, that I am an introvert. But the test deemed me so by only about 52 percent. I'm very close to the middle. I enjoy group outings and doing things with other people, just as much as I enjoy being alone. I need balance. I said that to say, someone who more heavily favors either side would likely have a different perspective on being alone. The key is that no matter where we fall on the spectrum, we find value in our moments of internal reflection. The amount of time that is needed for such self-care varies from person to person.

I get why being and doing things alone might sound horrible and like something no one can enjoy in truth. There is plenty of research out there to support the idea that humans are wired for connection. We're also led to view the state of aloneness as something abnormal. However, I'm about to make a case for it.

A couple of years ago, I took a solo trip to San Francisco for a conference. Since it was my first time visiting, I decided that I'd stay through the weekend and explore the city. I woke up each morning and walked to a little diner down the street from my hotel for food, rode a sightseeing tour bus around town, and visited a bunch of local attractions. It didn't take long for me to notice how freeing it all felt.

When you take trips with other people, there's always someone else you have to consider. Sometimes, you even have to completely concede to another person in order to avoid tension and ensure that you have an enjoyable time. It's important to be able to compromise and accommodate others. Anyone who doesn't know how or refuses to do this won't be much fun to be around. However, as an INFP-A "mediator" personality who is guided by principles and motivated by peace, I'm usually always the one doing the accommodating.

For those unfamiliar with the Myers-Briggs Type Indicator and the 16 Personalities test, according to its creators, here's what those letters stand for:

> **I** = Introverted: Prefers solitary activities. Exhausted by social interaction.
> **N** = Intuitive: Very Imaginative, open-minded, and curious.
> **F** = Feeling: Sensitive. More empathetic than competitive.
> **P** = Prospecting: Flexible, relaxed nonconformists.
> **A** = Assertive: Self-assured and even-tempered.

The mediator aspect represents an idealist always looking for the hint of good in even the worst of people and events, searching for ways to make things better. Now you should see why I'm frequently the person who relents to accommodating someone else. Not that we can't be as we choose regardless of how we're labeled, but my ultimate desire is always to maintain harmony.

I loved my solo exploration of San Francisco so much that I did it again when visiting Washington, D.C. for a seminar. I didn't even attempt to seek out other attendees to hang with. I thoroughly enjoyed sitting outside with breakfast and a book before the day's sessions began. During my downtime, I took another tour bus and got off at almost all of the national monuments, landmarks, and historical buildings. There were no stops skipped because someone else wasn't interested.

I stayed in museums as long as I wanted, until one of them closed. The only thing I didn't do was twirl through the halls. No one complained about feet hurting or being tired and ready to leave. Full tourist mode was activated. I even hopped on a rent-a-bike and cruised around downtown. I lingered, people-watched, and took tons of photos. Including some taken of me by nice people with whom I had engaging conversation. This was one of the best trip experiences I'd ever had.

Better to be alone than in bad company. Better to be in good company than alone.

I believe that message. So I won't pretend that doing things with other people always sucks. Even the greatest experiences can be made better when shared. But being and doing things alone shouldn't be viewed as a negative circumstance to be avoided. There are many pleasures to be derived from taking autonomous adventures.

When doing things alone, you can focus 100 percent on **you**, your needs and desires with no external interference. You can do what makes you happy and make decisions without having to consider the feelings of or consult with another. This is important because pouring into others without replenishing ourselves is how we end up trying to pour from empty cups. We need these times of self-indulgence for our mental and emotional well-being. Even if that time is spent doing nothing at all.

Focusing on yourself serves as a reminder that you matter. You see yourself as a whole person and are reminded of who you are independent of anyone else. In these moments, that person feels like enough. It's true that we teach people how to treat us. We have to make ourselves number one sometimes because constantly putting our desires on the back burner for others ensures that's where they'll stay.

I won't pretend it's all sunshine and freedom, however. No matter how comfortable you are alone, we all desire companionship sometimes and can get a bit dejected when it's unavailable. It's normal to long for someone with whom to share our life's journey. This is not a sign of weakness, but of humanity. I'm sure that even content and comfortable, self-proclaimed loners experience instances where solitude feels like confinement.

If nothing else prompts a desire to have a special someone or fellowship with other people, holidays will often get it done. These are times traditionally slated for loved ones to enjoy one another's company. Sitting at home alone eating a pizza while it seems everyone else is congregating for a barbeque or Thanksgiving dinner can be tough. If you do have family and friends to spend holidays with, then may come the wishing you had a partner to bring along, introduce to other important people in your life, share inside jokes, and trade stories with later.

It's not fun being the only single person in every room, especially when others take it upon themselves to make it a topic of conversation. In general, people want to know, where's your man? Family asks when they'll get to come to your wedding. Mom wants to know when you'll give her some grandbabies. No one asks about your career plans or other life ambitions. Maybe as a footnote, but it's never the main topic of conversation.

Sitting through endless questions and deflecting unwarranted hook-up attempts can be exasperating, even if you're happy in your current state. Then you get the couples who are all over each other and leave you feeling as though you're invading their privacy, witnessing something you shouldn't, but there's no place else to go.

We haven't even gotten into the physical deficiencies that can result from being alone. Physical touch is an actual communicator of love. According to Dr. Gary Chapman, author of *The 5 Love Languages*, it's directly correlated to the ability of some to identify with the emotion. Not to mention that it feels good and is relaxing and comforting. The effects of lacking in this area cannot be overstated.

There are essential elements of our existence that are fulfilled through companionship, relationship, and social interaction. This is why being alone is tough for some people and a situation many flat-out avoid. It can feel empty, as though something is lacking. It tests your patience, it tries your will, and it challenges your resolve. And yes, being alone can get very lonely. It's difficult at times. We don't have to pretend that it's not so that others won't assume this is our default state.

Balance is the key. Everything in moderation: alone time, socializing, even moderation itself. But being alone is far from the worst thing in the world.

Often, in being more inclined to embark on solo outings, you remember how much you enjoy things that you haven't been able to do in a while because no one wanted to do them with you. It's great if others are sure to consider your feelings and make your desires a priority. But that should be a bonus to the love and consideration that you show yourself. If you continuously defer to others, trust that they will come to expect it and possibly even take advantage of you.

When in a relationship, I still take time for myself. It's not that I don't enjoy the company of my partner. I love doing things as a couple. It's just that time for yourself actually helps keep a relationship healthy. It gives you space to miss and appreciate the other person. It can be the difference between supporting one another and being codependent.

I've even gone to concerts alone on occasion because no one else in my circle was a fan of the particular artist. That may be the one that takes a little getting used to. Music by nature is a medium that brings people together, creating a communal atmosphere. Both dancing and singing along with the band are definitely more fun and less awkward when you're with someone. The thing is, once the show starts it's fine. Alone or not, I always feel like I'm just there for the music. I get lost in it. The fellowship is secondary.

No one ever asks about this though. When I return from these solo excursions, friends inquire mostly about whether I met someone or had a one-night-stand. They want to know about the men who were in attendance, and scoff at my indifference. I guess what was learned or seen isn't nearly as fascinating when you're single.

I don't think any preconceived notions about being single bother me more than this one. It's the assumption of loneliness that leads to the assumption of desperation and most of the other unattractive labels. Being lonely entails aching and sadness. None of the experiences I recounted involve this. Yet, people will look at you with concern and even a bit of pity when you mention having done something alone that is typically a common group activity. Not much gets to me, but the avoidance of that moment does sometimes make me hesitant to mention it at all.

It can get out of hand what people expect you to put up with in order to evade loneliness. I'll never be the girl who chooses a man over my sanity and sense of self-worth. Nor will I be the girl who views being miserable in any relationship as more desirable than being content and alone. Because it's not.

So, no, being single is not synonymous with being lonely. There is too much life to be lived to wallow in self-pity simply because you are not attached to a partner. Searching for your worth in others will always leave you short. There are benefits to being single and things to be enjoyed. Many, especially those on the outside, just can't see or understand the advantages.

There is this inner calm, this quiet delight that comes from doing things alone. There is no one to please, no negative energy or bad vibes. There is minimal dialogue. You can immerse yourself in thought or be captivated by surrounding beauty. You learn so much about yourself, who you are and what you like. Then, in feeding your soul these things and making personal joy a priority, you learn how to love yourself.

Anyone who has never enjoyed being single is doing it wrong. This is not to say that other people are unnecessary or expendable. I've covered how essential human interaction is to personal development. It's just, a woman who is alone shouldn't be automatically labeled "lonely." The single woman has her friends, she has her career, her aspirations, and most importantly, she has herself.

I know, I know . . . none of those things can wrap their arms around and keep you warm at night. Yet, this one seemingly missing piece should not overshadow all the others that are present, and pertinent.

Single.

THAT DOES NOT MEAN JEALOUS

I'd bet everything I own on the idea that every woman who's been single for any significant period of time has been accused of being jealous of someone's relationship. It doesn't matter how unhealthy and unappealing the relationship is, for some reason, you're thought to be envious. The involved individuals assume, and more scarily believe, that the single woman covets what they have. Because having a terrible someone is better than having no one. Right?

I sometimes think people want you to be jealous because it makes them feel better about themselves or their relationship. So they convince themselves that this is the case as a means of self-gratification. The idea of someone wanting what you have makes the relationship, him, or her more desirable. People will blatantly try to get a reaction out of you. Ever been around someone who randomly brings up something their significant other did, or continually gushes about the person even if out of context? Like, when you say, "I'm hungry," this person responds with "so-and-so is hungry all the time." I mean, what is that? Then when you grow annoyed or call out the absurdity, you're accused of being jealous.

Not always, of course. When you really like a guy or are falling in love, you just want to talk about him all the time because you're thinking about him. There's not always an underlying motive. But sometimes there is, and you can often tell the difference.

Unfortunately, accusations of jealousy also frequently follow advice or opinion offered to, but not well received by a romantically involved friend. It's sad, really. Oftentimes you're telling this friend the truth about her situation out of love and concern. Yet, because you are single, it's taken as something else. It's taken as you wanting to disband the couple so that your friend can be single like you. It's taken as you being miserable and wanting your friend to be miserable with you. It's taken as you being jealous. Why else would you be out here trying to break up an (un)happy home?

This goes back to that warped perception of being single as the most undesirable state for a woman. I've heard men speak of it as though we are to avoid such a fate like it's a personal extinction-level event. I have heard women chastised for listening to their *single friends* and threatened with the idea of ending up *like them*. How frightening, to be single rather than treated poorly in a demeaning, disrespectful relationship.

It works, too. We've established this hierarchy where for a woman, any romantic relationship, including those deeply flawed and personally detrimental is ranked above being alone. We're told that a male partner who cheats is just a "man being a man." As long as he comes home to us it doesn't matter the sins committed while away. I've heard the mention, on several occasions, of being the one he comes home to used in defense by women against others who have lain with their men.

I find myself wondering if I'm really *that* different because I sincerely don't get it. I don't ever intend to judge, I just honestly view this as a peculiar concept. My perception and thought process can't be that rare. I just cannot fathom the idea that we have put men on such a higher platform that we feel more inferior not having one than being partnered with a man who doesn't hold us or the concept of agreed-upon monogamy in high regard.

When I say "we" I mean the collective culture. I know there's more to it than self-esteem or women being lonely. We didn't simply decide that this is acceptable. It's just been ingrained into our psyche, both overtly and subliminally. Every time we see a damsel in distress in a movie or a woman applauded for standing by her habitually embarrassing husband, the concept is reinforced. Women didn't invent the rules. We do, however, play by them. At some point, as we allow the narrative to continue and even feed into it, we imply consent.

That is what's most disheartening, the fact that us women often "drink this Kool-Aid." We've allowed ourselves to accept a disproportionate allocation of value. That's exactly what we're doing by operating within a social construct that has instilled within us the belief that the opposite sex is to be allowed certain freedoms and held to different standards based solely on their gender—without diminishing their worth in the process.

We accept this ideology under the guise that "nobody is perfect." Well that's very true. No human being is perfect. However, this is not an excuse to engage in or accept willful shenanigans. It's certainly not enough to support a flawed theory that your single friend is jealous of a relationship.

I won't make this a one-sided assessment. Perhaps the relationship is healthy overall. So there is legitimate concern that your single friend who may have had something negative to say *is* jealous that she doesn't have this in her life. There are absolutely situations where this can be the case. My point is don't strip away her allowance to have an unbiased opinion simply because she is single. Don't allow that sole factor to determine motive. A woman can be single while happy for and supportive of a friend who has found love. These two events are not mutually exclusive.

There are different forms of jealousy. Maybe you don't think your single friend is jealous of the relationship, but that this other person is taking you away from her. It is definitely an adjustment. If you've been close friends who do everything together, go everywhere together, and talk constantly throughout the day, this sudden change can take some getting used to. That is to be respected. Be patient and gentle with your still-single friend. Don't diminish her behavior and hurt feelings to simple bitterness. As a friend who has been there for you, loved you, cared for you, and accepted you, she deserves better.

It will probably help if the single friend feels as though time is still made for the relationship and she hasn't been completely cast aside. Feeling as though space is being saved for her can go a long way toward softening the blow of loosening that connection. If the concern is not there to continue nurturing that bond, it can appear as though she was taken for granted or only a placeholder until a romantic partner came along.

Sometimes, our vision of everything and everyone else is obscured when all we see is butterflies. We want to do everything and spend every free moment with our significant other. So we have to consciously make sure we don't completely stop hanging out with friends in favor of doing so. If you consider the friendship important (and you should if this has been a long-time, close relationship), then plan outings for just the two of you. Don't turn down every invitation she extends. The involved friend can't always dictate the terms of when and how time will be spent.

When you're single, people tend to suppose that you're always available. Yet, it can be a struggle to get those same people to do anything you ask of them. Having a significant other can cause one to severely underestimate the importance of friendships. We can't forget who was there for us before a partner came into our lives, and who will be there still, if they go. Single and involved women may have different interests, but it's important to find some common ground.

Be thankful for that friend who cares enough to notice your absence, and is true enough to be honest with you, even when she knows you won't like what she has to say. Maybe the person she called a dirtbag is actually a dirtbag! Trust that it is much easier to smile, lie, and say what a person wants to hear when you aren't emotionally invested in her well-being. Most of the time she's candid because she's concerned.

Jealousy is a natural human emotion when experienced with temperance. Too much of anything becomes toxic. But if this is not the case, don't be so quick to assume that a single woman is envious of any romantic relationship. Maybe she has no issue with being single and therefore none with the opposite. Maybe she's actually happy. Even if she's not, and desires to be in a relationship herself, don't think so little of her that you believe she would allow this to poison her thoughts or negatively influence her decisions. It's not the basis for all that she is, feels, says, and does.

Single.

THAT DOES NOT MEAN SEXUALLY
FRUSTRATED

Exact words in a message I received from a guy I was never friends with or had even met in person:

"Camey . . .

you need some good DICK . . . which will inspire you to write a different kinda book."

He wrote this in a group chat. I was in there along with some mutual friends, all of whom were men, but he and I didn't know each other outside of the chat. Someone else in the group had upset him. So he called himself "signing off" before exiting the chat room and that was his farewell message to me.

Being that I don't know this guy, I believe it a safe assumption to say that his message was based solely on the fact that I was single. And maybe because I never responded to his or anyone else's advances. I never opened the door for him or others in the room to give me the good "loving" I apparently needed so desperately.

Perhaps he would have reacted this way no matter my relationship status. Such a random outburst says more about his view of women than it does about me. Clearly, he views women as here for the pleasure of men. He didn't see me as a person, not really. Not someone with qualities to offer independent of my sexual orientation. To him, a woman has one use that trumps all others in significance, and this must be fulfilled for us to be whole. Evidently, good dick cures all. It's even a source of inspiration.

Books such as *Fifty Shades of Grey*, erotica, and others revolving around sex, or at least with some steamy love-making scenes can be a source of great storytelling. I get that part. Sex sells. It's engaging and exciting. There's one word in particular that stands out in his message though, and ruins the entire notion. Vulgarity of his expression aside, the word "need" is the issue.

There are a couple of things wrong with this: First, the assumption that I am not sexually satisfied. Second, that I write self-help, inspirational books and articles for this reason. It can't be because I want to and actually enjoy writing in this genre. Couldn't be that helping others helps me. Nah. I write those types of books because I haven't had the kind of sex that would inspire me to put pen to paper and sing its praises.

I was actually dating someone seriously at the time. Having good sex regularly, and I was completely content. His small mind just never considered that possibility because I hadn't slept with him or anyone he knew. This is silly. It's an "if I don't know, it doesn't happen" approach. It's a delusional and ridiculous attitude. As is the assumption that if a woman is not interested in sleeping with you, there's something wrong with her and she's not having sex with anyone. It doesn't get much more pompous and self-absorbed than that.

Clearly, sex is his motivator. Sex is a lot of people's motivator, which is one of my biggest turnoffs. Enjoy it, desire it, but don't let sexual desire guide you. It will set you up for failure every time. It's a turnoff for me because I feel it shows a lack of discipline and authenticity. These are your serial cheaters. If decisions are made about others and your own behavior based solely on the desire for sex, it's a license to avoid practicing restraint and respect.

Then there are those men who behave a certain way and pretend to be exactly what a woman wants to get her into bed. Naturally, when sex is a motivator that person will do just about whatever is necessary to satisfy the craving. It's always his number one goal. It's actually kind of sad. Men miss out on incredible women who they never care to learn about in earnest when this is always their primary objective.

For some men, a woman who he is not sleeping with and cannot sleep with in the future is of no value. I was a woman for whom that guy had no use. So, in his signing off, he didn't care at all about being rude or dismissive. He said exactly what he likely had been thinking for a while, not caring if it would offend me, knowing that we'd likely never speak again. It was basically a middle finger to the woman who would never sleep with him. Because what else could I have to offer?

I must be completely transparent and note that the guy did apologize later, after his friends got on him about the incident. It was an apology nonetheless. He tried to fix it. He said that he meant no harm and mentioned the quality of my writing and how he'd love to read that same passion in a book about love.

It's not what you say. Well, sometimes it is. Most times it's more about how, when, and why you say it. It's about the tone and implied sentiment. He couldn't have communicated his alleged idea any worse.

Let's start unraveling this attempt at reasoning by addressing the insinuation that good dick would make me write a book about love. These are two separate circumstances. Any adult who has dated at all knows that sex and love are not the same. They can complement one another, but each can also exist without the other. Thinking that because a man makes passionate love *to* you means that he's in love *with* you is a heinous mistake that I'm sure most women have made at some point. But we quickly learn this lesson.

Love is love. Sex is sex. Sometimes the two intersect and we create something beautiful. But one can never assume that because someone leaves us physically satisfied that there are deeper feelings attached. I know this. I'm sure the guy knows this. So his explanation falls apart right there. He said what he said, and what he meant, even if only in that moment.

His raw, uninhibited thoughts did not reflect my accolades or intellect. They spoke only to sexual objectivity. It was like, yeah you write but so what if it's not related to something we actually want to hear you talk about. His approach suggested that my topic endeavors outside of intimacy are cultivated out of necessity. It is a perception of women that has to connect them to sex somehow.

Since I don't really know this guy I can't say if he's good or bad. I can't attest to the type of man or even human being that he is. Also, I understand that people sometimes act out of character when they are upset. He was lashing out in that goodbye message, and not just at me. I do believe I was simply caught in the crossfire.

It was just odd that he brought me, a person he doesn't actually know into the text assault, and that's what he chose to say. However, it's not that surprising. People generally believe that single, independent, strong-willed women aren't getting enough action. They make it synonymous with being a bitch, and to be cured, we just need a good old-fashioned roll in the sheets—a heavy dose of dick.

I went on a trip for work once, along with a male colleague. We went to a convention out of state. Upon checking into our adjoining rooms, I closed the connecting door and that's how it stayed pretty much the entire time. I saw no reason to have it open. I was not romantically drawn to him and am a proponent of not sending mixed messages or presenting opportunities for unwarranted advances. I wanted to keep things fun and friendly between us, but professional.

As the trip was winding down, one day he knocked on said door. I opened it and he proceeded to ask why I'd kept it closed. Before I could answer he chuckled and called me "A" sexual. For those unfamiliar, asexuality is the lack of sexual attraction to others, or low or absent interest in, or desire for sexual activity.

That's when it dawned on me that he believed we might have sex while away on this business trip. I barely knew this guy, had only met him just a few months prior. Why would he think that? Because he's a man and I'm a woman? There was literally no other reason or indication to believe this might transpire. But since I clearly was not concerned with having sex, there was something wrong with me. Because I was not sexually attracted to him, I must not be sexually attracted to anyone. The nerve! The ego. The recurring theme of pompous self-absorption.

The thing is, I may have found him attractive. It was so long ago that I don't really remember. It just doesn't matter. I'm not so hard up for sex that I jump on every remotely appealing option. Especially when the option is basically a stranger, *and* a colleague. I also believe he had a girlfriend at the time.

Plus, I'm very disciplined. I consider it one of my greatest strengths as it makes for viable impulse control. Rule yourself or you'll lose yourself is my personal mantra. You can't succumb to every fleeting desire or emotion if you hope to have any control over your life. Even if the guy was attractive and single and engaged, that doesn't automatically mean the door between us would've been left open as an invitation.

I don't place great weight on being found sexually desirable. Sure, I appreciate compliments. I just don't enjoy being reduced to them. Like anyone else I want to be considered attractive by the gender that I am attracted to. It matters. I take the time to do my hair, select the perfect outfit, and look my best when I go out mostly for my own self-confidence, but of course attention from others is a factor. I won't lie and pretend that I don't care at all. To feel desired is something we all crave. But all attention isn't good attention or welcomed.

To be admired only for my appearance is not admiration at all. It's objectification. Mere things display the entirety of their value on the surface. We can look at a couch and say it's pretty, or a bracelet and think it's cute, and have that be all that it is. We even refer to cars as sexy. But humans are complex beings with layers of unique details. To reduce the worth of a woman to only what she looks like is not a compliment.

This is a matter of taste. Different women en-joy different things and have varying levels of com-fort. It's important to find out where each individual stands. You can offend one woman with the same things another enjoyed. I don't speak for all women— just myself and those like me who can appreciate flirting and flattery in appropriate context, but ulti-mately wish to be viewed as all that we are.

Sex isn't my motivator mainly because it's so easy to get and most of the time is meaningless. There is a place for casual encounters. But I'll never be moved by anything so common and insincere. It's like being driven to spend $40,000 on a picture of a BMW. Even if it's the best picture ever taken, it's not some-thing to be *that* invested in obtaining. That money could have been spent on the real thing. Show me something genuine, some depth, and you'll have my attention.

I know there is a distinct difference between lust and genuine connection or love. I haven't only run into these kinds of issues with casual acquaintances, but also in my dating life. My views don't change to suit the circumstance. Someone else may fool me but I seldom will fool myself!

In the beginning stages of dating someone, I'm rarely all-in. I'm in "wait and see" mode, not from a place of pessimism or negativity but with the understanding that lust looks a lot like love, feels like it, too. And in the beginning, before you've really gotten to know someone, who they are, what they stand for, and if the two of you are compatible, it's *all* lust. That is, unless you believe in the very, very unusual phenomenon of love at first sight. Rather than dive right into the deep end as soon as I meet someone new, I just put my feet in the water, enjoy the process, and observe.

I've had guys make assumptions that I'm not an affectionate person because I'm not all over them after the first couple of dates. This is always puzzling to me because I'm like, we literally just became acquainted. Sometimes being unfamiliar with one another is cool, depending on what you're looking for. But to make that kind of judgment or assess the intimacy level of a relationship so early on seems strange to me. We are the most intelligent species to ever exist, yet often we allow our primal instincts to cancel out that intelligence.

On the other side of that, when someone is all over *me* or claims to like me so much and wants to be in a relationship before even really knowing who I am, it feels fake. It can't be genuine because there is no basis for such a position, other than lust or infatuation. You can crush on me, but if there is little attempt to actually learn about me, then you don't like me. Not really. You can't. You don't know me. You just like how I look or are drawn to some other nonessential element of my being, such as a cute laugh or the shape of my eyes. Fascination with such things will eventually fade. They get old and common. There has to be something more meaningful beneath fringe attraction for it to last.

Lust gets a bad rep, though. It is an intricate component of romantic love. A relationship with no level of physical attraction and passion is in trouble. Or, it's a friendship. Even Osho, an enlightened philosopher explains in his book *Love, Freedom, Aloneness* that in avoiding lust, we avoid the possibility of love itself. He's careful to mention that love is not lust, but love is not *without* lust. The first part of that statement is what gives lust its negative connotation. It is because we confuse it with love, and in doing so attach expectations that inevitably aren't met and ill-fitting emotions that cause us to view lust as something wicked. As with any other impulse, we just have to exercise discipline and practice sound decision-making.

It's often lust alone that breaks our hearts or disappoints us, not love. Lust manipulates, confuses, and lies to us. That's why it's important that we learn the difference.

If the intensity of the interaction fluctuates, a partner is hot and cold, you're always wondering how he feels about you, or there's lots of sex but little conversation or anything else, then you're almost certainly in lust. That's close to a no-brainer, no matter what the butterflies in your tummy try to tell you. You shouldn't feel discarded, used, or forgotten. Same thing if you find yourself doing the discarding and forgetting. Love is consistent. It may falter but it does not fail.

The most tried-and-tested method is to just give the situation time before deciding what it is. We can be in such a rush to fall in love that we create it in places and with people where it does not exist. True colors always show eventually. If someone isn't sincerely interested in you as a person, not just as an object of desire, they'll tire of trying to woo you. Let them. Sometimes we feel pressured to give people what they want when they want it (including sex) for fear that they'll move on if we don't. Believe you're worth the wait and anyone worthy will believe it, too.

I'm not impressed by someone finding me a suitable lover. That's pure biology. I've grown better than I used to be at separating the two and recognizing the difference, both in others and myself. Mainly because I've learned that there is one, and I accept that realization even when doing so is hurtful.

I guess a single woman should always want sex with every man she encounters. I guess we need to take it where we can get it! Don't dare turn a man down if you're unattached. He'll take it personally, as though you're saying something is wrong with him. In turn, he'll convince himself that something is wrong with you. Not all men, of course. But this is a common tactic of those who judge a woman, and her sex life, based solely on her relationship status. Oh, and also those who make her sex life important enough to even pass judgment.

Single.

THAT DOES NOT MEAN UNREALISTIC

A common write-off for a woman who is single is that she wants too much and has unrealistic expectations of partners and relationships. First of all, how is there such a thing as "wanting too much?" You want what you want. And there is a monumental difference between compromise and settling.

Compromise is meeting in the middle. It is wavering on little things that are not critical to the foundation of the relationship. Settling is accepting what you know you don't want and what you know is not good for you just to be in a relationship. Or, you convince yourself that you do want whatever it is.

Though it can be a factor, settling is not always a product of poor self-perception. I know people who think very highly of themselves. I believe I have an elevated perception of myself. Yet, there are times when each of us has settled for less than we felt was deserved or desired. This is a universal challenge. I think we've all been faced with the dilemma of accepting inferior or undesirable options versus waiting for something more ideal, and we don't always choose the latter no matter how esteemed our self-image may be.

Even people who love themselves sometimes settle, and there are many different motivations—too many to reduce it to the result of not caring for ourselves enough. If I were to think back on every time I may have acquiesced against my own heart and my better judgment, I can attribute doing so to one of several reasons.

Behavioral psychologists call the condition that keeps us from fulfillment, "habituation." This

means that given enough experience with circumstances through repeated exposures over time, we
become accustomed to things as they are. Our response to the stimulus decreases. We accept that this is
just how life is and the extent of what is available to
us. This is our relationship, these are our friends, this
is our job, etc. Situations become absolutes and
mainstays based on no other logic than this is how it's
always been.

The reason could be based in fear, which often
influences many of our decisions. We make the safe
choice and place the sure bet; afraid to venture past
our comfort zones and let go of certainties because we
aren't sure what else is out there for us. The unknown
can be frightening. Yet, it can also be exhilarating. The
idea that there exists an abundance of possibilities we
have yet to explore should be encouraging.

We stay in unhealthy, unfulfilling relationships
for fear that we may not find anyone else. When if we
stop to think about it, someone new always comes
along. Always. There may be a spell of loneliness and
heartache to endure, but sooner or later we'll meet
someone and carry on with our lives. We'll form
another relationship, hopefully with lessons in tow
that we learned from the last.

When we do go for things and are not success-ful or have a bunch of bad dates and negative experi-ences in love, it can shake our belief. This is another reason that we settle. We can have complete confi-dence that we are worthy of all that we seek, but the trust that it's out there and will come to us wavers after futile attempts. In these moments it's important that we not only believe we're worth what we desire, but also the wait necessary to obtain it. We owe it to ourselves to endure the loneliness and whatever other struggles may come while bringing our vision to fruition.

We just get tired sometimes. I know I do. We grow weary of fighting, failing, believing, trying, and hoping. It becomes easier to settle for what we have when we can't find the energy to continue pursuing something greater. Rest is essential to our mental and emotional health. We just can't quit, which usually goes hand-in-hand with settling. Instead, let's take breaks. Do nothing, relax, and recharge. Take a dating hiatus rather than give in to more fruitless relation-ships. Energy always replenishes itself eventually. How disappointing it would be to regain strength after committing to a situation we're certain we don't want to be in.

The lesser talked about reason for our settling is a lack of self-preparation. We have to put ourselves in position to attain those things we say that we want and be the type of person we wish to attract. We have to do the work—on ourselves and in our lives. This could involve going to therapy or anything else that contributes to our becoming the best version of ourselves and brings us closer to our goals. We can't cheat the process. Unfortunately, sometimes we end up settling because we're expecting maximum results with minimal effort and leave ourselves little choice.

Prepare yourself. Do the work and trust the process. Then, find the courage to act on the belief that what you deserve and desire is not only out there, but will come to you. No matter how old we grow or how long we've been single, we should never feel as though settling for unappealing options is our only available course of action. Even when we feel deserted, afraid, frustrated, disappointed, and defeated, it's important to trust that whatever we want is attainable. It may not come when we hope for it. We may think we have it and then be proven wrong. Our mental, physical, and emotional vitality may wane. None of that means our waiting will be in vain. We'll never know though, if we throw in the towel on our journey.

There is no limit on how long we're allowed to have our desired level of established criteria, nor how high we can set the bar. This seems pretty standard. Yet, it's astonishing how people can view standards in dating as a bad thing and actually encourage you to lower them. They'll tell you that you're never going to find anyone unless you do. Like the guy from my story earlier, who assumed I was looking for the perfect, nonexistent man.

I don't have some checklist of inconsequential characteristics that I compare against men I meet. I do, however, have a general idea of things that I will not accept. Deception, as well as a lack of integrity and/or discipline are things for which I have an extremely low tolerance. You only have to exhibit these traits once or twice for me to move on, as I don't believe any are present in a healthy relationship. There's no reason I should be open to such behavior. But really, that's it. I don't have anything even close to an exhaustive catalog of must-have attributes.

Now, I must say that I've grown. Before, I did weigh things such as height and vehicle requirements more heavily than I should have. I treated preferences like needs. The more I dated, I was able to learn what matters and what doesn't. I even started consciously dating outside of my type.

I've learned the hard way that having set criteria in dating doesn't necessarily yield more favorable results. Someone may meet our every requirement, allowing us to check every single box on our wish list, and the relationship will still crumble. That's if it ever comes together in the first place.

In dating outside of my type, I started by stripping away those superficial qualities that I considered when deciding whether or not to engage. Dating men who are shorter than me, who don't have a vehicle, or make a certain amount of money are only a few that I've deliberately addressed. The idea behind the last two standards is not to be a snob, but stems from value given to being paired with an equal— someone who is at least in a position comparable to my own. However, what I'd been neglecting is the fact that life happens.

We fall on hard times beyond our control. I'd hope that unfortunate circumstances weren't held against me if I were in such a situation. Sometimes people may just take a little longer than you to get where they're going. Current condition isn't always indicative of future status. A person may have the means, but doesn't feel the need to own a vehicle in our era of ridesharing apps. Perhaps for some, being passionate about a job takes precedence over how much it pays. These are all viable reasons for not meeting particular benchmarks that don't automatically make an individual less worthwhile.

I want to be careful with this because we can get ourselves into trouble by dating potential. We often end up setting impractical expectations and are left sorely disappointed. Also, I think that it can be to our benefit sometimes to simply take a break from dating while we work on ourselves. If we know that we don't have much at the moment to bring to a relationship or add to another person, it may best to just remain single and get our personal houses in order. It doesn't hurt to get to know someone though, and learn whether or not they're motivated, hardworking, responsible, and focused enough to realize that potential. It's the difference between making a preemptive or informed decision.

For every time that I've been satisfied by the results of doing this, there has been an instance where I was reminded of how incompatible I am with certain personalities. But I still believe it's worth it. I don't want to turn down the person who would ride the bus to bring me flowers for the one who'll hop into his fancy car in the middle of the night and drive right out of my life.

I've also started to date people who I may not be overwhelmingly physically attracted to at first. Sometimes we know exactly what our type consists of, other times it's more subconscious. We just somehow continue to select or attract similar partners over and over again without stopping to connect the dots and realize what they all have in common. Some may have a more extensive list of preferences than others, but we each have specific traits to which we're drawn. I'm 100 percent aware that height is one of mine. Tall and lanky? Here's my number. And my heart.

So, maybe if the guy who accused me of having unrealistic standards would have met me a few years earlier, he would've been right. He would have hit the nail on the head. It still would have been nothing more than a lucky guess however, a stereotype even.

For a single woman, standards are suddenly viewed as deterrents. This is why we're single, of course. The reason is that we won't just accept whoever is willing to offer commitment. How dare we actually have an idea of what we want from a relationship, how we wish to be treated, and stick to that? When we have someone who considers himself a perfectly fine mate, and he very well may be, right in front of us, not being interested is mindboggling.

We set unattainable benchmarks sometimes. Yes. We also have perhaps crafted grand ideas of love and relationships from movies like *The Notebook*. I mean, who wouldn't want to experience that kind of rare, unbounded adoration? Each of us has likely been in a situation where we were looking for what amounts to perfection. That is until we really come to grips with the fact that we're not perfect. As hard as we try, no one will ever be every single thing that another person wants. It's unfair to expect this of someone. Such a goal is unachievable, and I imagine the pressure is debilitating.

I also came to understand that nobody owes anybody anything. Not attention, not time, not reciprocity, not even love. We don't like to hear that because it doesn't seem fair. Nonetheless, we must allow others the choice to offer us these things or not. Sometimes they will, sometimes they won't. We don't have to maintain the relationship or like the outcome, but we must accept it and proceed accordingly. Presenting our wants and needs as obligations to be met will lead to inauthentic actions performed with reluctance, often leading to resentment.

The repetitive theme of unwarranted assumptions is the problem here. It is the belief that a single woman should lower herself to the level on which others have placed her in order to snag a man. She's allowed to want what she wants, as others want what they want. She is no less justified than anyone else in aiming to build the kind of relationship she imagines. And anyone who cannot or will not give those things to her should leave her be.

There is no shame in being incapable of meeting her needs. The disgrace is in trying to convince her that she is too much when the reality is that the other party, for her, is not enough. And that's okay. It's important to know who we are and who we are not without being compelled to paint someone else in a negative light as a defense mechanism.

As a single woman, there is nothing automatically erroneous about your desires. If you are that person you hope to encounter, if you embody those qualities, and give what you aim to receive, then you know the idea exists—because you exist. It can't possibly be unrealistic. You're real. Therefore, it is also real.

Single.

THAT DOES NOT MEAN HIGH
MAINTENANCE

People who are high maintenance demand a lot of attention. They're considered hard to please and sometimes even needy. The simple things aren't really their thing. You know that when you're with a high maintenance partner you might have to put in a lot of work to keep them content while in the relationship.

Sometimes it's an overwhelming, tiring amount of work. Or you may just need to give partners space and support to be able to offer themselves the attention they need.

A man may just have to learn to let his lady spend inordinate amounts of time at the nail salon, spa, or hairstylist without flipping out. A woman may need to try and be less critical of her man's penchant for self-grooming and spending money on expensive colognes or designer shoes. Even better, each could find something to do with any extra time they'll have to themselves. Enjoy the few hours of freedom!

Indulgences can offer a confidence boost or much needed psychological decompression. You feel good about yourself when you look in the mirror wearing a well-tailored suit or stylish new haircut. Behavior that may be considered to signal that a person is high maintenance doesn't have to strain a relationship. Sometimes, the other involved party only need not stand in the way.

I had one guy tell me on a date that he doesn't like pretty women because they're high maintenance. "I don't like pretty women . . ." was odd enough before he completed the statement. He then went on to comment on my designer bag and how "we" like to spend exorbitant amounts of money on things like that.

Little did he know, I'd had that bag for years and actually got it highly discounted from a store like T.J. Maxx. That's beside the point though. Wherever and whenever I got the bag, I paid for it. And even if I hadn't, that was a hugely premature leap. Did I mention this was our second meeting?

It was the first time I'd been knowingly adversely stereotyped for what are generally considered desirable qualities, such as being found attractive. When I countered with him being a gamer, spending hundreds of dollars on consoles, equipment, and video games, he just smirked. He didn't care. He'd already decided, I'm single; I'm "pretty"; I must be pretentious.

Now if a woman is a bit high maintenance, that's nothing of which to be ashamed. It's neither a negative nor positive. It's a personal preference. A woman should do what she does and like what she likes for herself, not to appease someone else. We have to get more comfortable with doing whatever makes us happy without feeling guilty or being concerned that it is wrong somehow. This is within reason, of course.

Too often, we try to squeeze into another person's mold and fit a preconceived image. In the process, we suppress parts of ourselves in order to be the ideal woman for a man. The result, though we may snag the guy, is almost always chronic unhappiness. It is nearly impossible to experience authentic joy when we ourselves aren't being genuine and living in truth. In terms of things that make us feel good but may bother someone else, there are much worse pursuits than lavish shoes and extra attention.

Plus, some men actually enjoy catering to a woman and being challenged to please. It makes them feel useful and appreciated. Some men just enjoy putting a smile on your face. Whatever that entails, they want to have a role in making a woman feel good. If we gauge good and bad traits based on reception, then that requirement is met here as well, as it is not always unwelcoming. This guy didn't like it but there are many out there who do.

In my situation, it was that the high maintenance theory was crafted based on little or no evidence and carried a negative connotation. Like "yeah, that's why you're single." You're too demanding and men have to break their backs to make you happy.

That's what this guy was saying. He came into our meeting searching with intent for the mysterious reason for my being unattached, looked at my bag, and conjured this epiphany. He was so smug about it, too. So proud of himself for not being lured by the effects of my high maintenance ways.

I want to touch on that phrase as well. People say "that's why you're single" as though it's some kind of disease. There's really this perception that being single is something awful to endure. I can't be bullied or shamed into shrinking by the use of my relationship status as an insult.

Back to the guy who sexualized EVERY-THING and spent insane amounts of money on gaming consoles and products, but held on to the nerve to roll his eyes at my (discount) designer handbag. I couldn't even say that I was going to take a bath without him offering a condescending laugh and reference to my being a tease in return. It was like dude, I have to wash my body. How else can I say it that won't come across suggestive?

He was either emotionally immature or very full of himself, perhaps both. Seriously, it got to the point where I had to choose ordinary words and the mention of mundane activities carefully so that he wouldn't decide to take it out of context. Somehow he still found a way. Clearly, he was likely the one with obvious hindrances keeping him single. Yet, he was more concerned with my potential shortcomings. Never mind that focusing on one's self, the only person who we can change, is infinitely more productive.

I am probably one of the least high maintenance women he'd ever met. I think that life is all about the little things, the thoughtful things. I also enjoy nice things. But I'd much rather spend $300 on an experience than a purse. He just saw what he wanted to see in order to complete his misguided storyline.

I'm a go-with-the-flow person who really doesn't ask for much. In fact, I've only recently gotten comfortable with letting people buy and do things for me. I always hit the clearance racks first when out shopping and am not an excessive spender. Maybe I would be if I had more money to throw away. But as of now, dropping $100 on a discount handbag is what I consider splurging.

I do practice self-care and am sure to treat myself on occasion. I have a nice car and condo, living in a quiet, middle-class neighborhood. I won't pretend that I'm a minimalist by any means. However, any of my closest friends can recount stories of their exasperation with my sometimes unnecessary frugalness. They'll tell you how I've lamented over whether or not to purchase a twenty-dollar shirt that I really wanted, and how they've intervened with an unsubtle nudge to "just get it!" Haha. I think this hesitancy to buy needless items even if I have the funds stems from having grown up poor.

My family never had much but it always felt like enough. With food on the table, clothes on our backs, and a roof over our heads, I didn't feel as though I lacked anything as a child. My basic needs were met without fail. I noticed that others might have had *nicer* things, but didn't equate that with them having more than I did.

My friends at school wore the latest designer shoes and jackets. Some of their parents even drove Cadillac's and other luxury vehicles, while we went through rounds of used cars. We had a car though. I guess for me, the absence of a deficiency was sufficient enough to camouflage the financial status of my family. That is until I was made aware by some of those same friends alerting me to the fact that I lived in "the projects." Or what you call low-income housing.

From then on I knew. And as I started to get older and wanted more things, I saw. Now I think part of me fears finding myself in this place once more, forced to accept misfortune. My thought process during purchasing decisions doesn't always stem from whether or not I can afford whatever it is, but this underlying caution to spend money that I finally have. I don't want to be poor again.

In my logical mind I know that spending twenty dollars on a shirt won't lead to this on its own. If it does then my problems are much bigger and I should just get the shirt anyway to bring myself a moment of comfort! But you'd be surprised at the random forcefulness with which anxiety can surface. It's not a rational perspective.

The irony is that a humble upbringing has also influenced me at points in my life to stretch myself beyond my means in order to avoid telling someone that I was broke. I didn't want anyone to know. I tried to keep up with people above my pay grade for appearances. I became hypersensitive about being pitied or perceived as impoverished, even if it were true. Two sides of the same coin—I'm either trying not to look poor, within reason, or trying not to *be* poor.

But overall, I'm pretty simple. Not even close to the pretentious persona that was implied during this date. I take pride in my appearance but am makeup-less most of the time and just as comfortable in sneakers as high heels, maybe more so. The fact that

I'm even compelled to say this and defend myself against a false narrative demonstrates how maddening these stereotypical situations can be.

It's one thing to deem someone incompatible, but it's quite another to do so based on an assessment that is incorrect. I don't expect to be everyone's type. Though rejection is uncomfortable for us all, I don't take it personally. I'd rather not be given a reason for it than subjected to one that someone decided to use without consideration for its validity.

I believe that he believed what he said though. He thought he was right. I'm sure of it. I only offered slight resistance. I'm not about to waste my time and energy trying to convince a person who has committed to misunderstanding me.

The truth is irrelevant when a determination has already been established about you. It's near impossible to change a made-up mind. And I don't know that we should want to change it. Someone who makes negative suppositions about us and holds on to them against reason, isn't the kind of person I'd like to be with in a romantic relationship. As one misconception is dispelled, I think these types of people eventually find another and another. You'll constantly be trying to prove yourself to them. No thanks.

A single woman is regularly up against the judgmental skepticism of others. We're combating small-minded, ill-informed ideologies and fixers who have us in their crosshairs. We find ourselves in circumstances that may make us feel as though we need to defend our position and status. Assessments of us are rarely fair or logical.

What happened to actually getting to know someone? Drawing hasty conclusions is lazy dating. Not to mention it's ineffective. It circumvents the process altogether as its only purpose is establishing satisfactory grounds to dismiss someone prematurely. This guy, like many others, just had to find something *wrong* with me, rather than get to know me. High maintenance was his fatal flaw of choice.

Single.

THAT DOES NOT MEAN BITTER

It's laughable how often I've heard being a single woman associated with also hating men. Laughable, though not at all funny. When you turn down advances and choose to remain single rather than embark on an undesirable, unfulfilling relationship, many believe it's because you have some type of grudge against the opposite sex. They want to know "who hurt you?"

The question doesn't come from a place of concern. It's a mocking of sorts that is said or implied with a condescending undertone. The sentiment is that something happened to make you this way. Someone cut you so deep that it ruined your potential. What a shame it is because you and whoever could have had something special if you weren't so damaged. That's the idea they try to wrap in less harsh packaging.

I've never really had my heart broken. Never been the victim of unfaithfulness (that I know of). I've had my feelings hurt, but I haven't experienced anything that would leave an internal scar of some kind, skew my perception of men, or cause me to harbor any unpleasant emotions toward them. I'm not triggered by the possibility of lies and deceit because this has not been a part of my dating and relationship endeavors.

The gift and the curse that has been my struggle in learning to be vulnerable has shielded me from such hurt. It's difficult to break a heart that's not fully open. I was raised in an environment that was not emotionally nurturing. My mother was young when she had me, learning not just how to be a parent to a child, but simply an adult. I spent a lot of time with my grandmother. She was a strict disciplinarian. Kids were seen and not heard. You didn't talk back, you listened. You weren't asked to do anything, you were told. How I felt or what I wanted was rarely, if ever considered.

I became guarded. I kept my feelings to myself for fear of them being dismissed, as they had been on many occasions. The only thing worse than the pain itself is feeling as though your pain has been invalidated.

We all develop coping mechanisms for trauma, some more healthy and effective than others. My self-preserving weapon of choice was detachment—from circumstances and people and their egregious actions. Though I wouldn't really call it a conscious choice. If we could just detach on command, we'd will ourselves to do it in every unbearable situation. For me, it just kind of happened. The more experience obtained with incidents that destroyed me inside, the better I became at not caring enough to allow this to happen. I got good at it, too good.

I saw myself on the outside of events that directly affected me. I wasn't concerned, not really. An empath at my core, I learned that I couldn't care if I wanted to survive.

I'm not sure how exactly I managed to be so far gone. I couldn't tell you how to do it. All I know is that I found myself here. I wouldn't call this space blissful, but it was quieter than the alternative. My perpetual state of detachment protected me from ruin in my younger years, but that cocoon became an obstacle as I grew into an adult.

As I got older, letting people all the way in felt uncomfortable. All of my relationships—friendly, romantic, or otherwise—existed only on the surface of my being. We could laugh, joke, and have a great time, but you'd never know me on a deeply personal level. This also allowed me to always have the upper hand in a relationship. I was never invested enough for the other person to be able to hurt me. If you're not being hurt, you can't be bitter.

Growing into a woman, I've learned that keeping people at arm's length and not fostering those deep connections makes it near impossible to build anything meaningful. And I wanted that. I began to make a cognizant effort to be more vulnerable without fear of the outcome. Until then, I'd had no particularly painful breakups.

I have no reason to be bitter. Men have been good to me. I've dated some gentlemen who were kind, considerate, and loving. I know the next question, where are these guys now? Well, someone can be an amazing person, but not a good partner for you. Sometimes we were just incompatible. Maybe we were at different places in life, with different mindsets and outlooks. Perhaps there was no chemistry. Sometimes there were simply no sustainable qualities upon which to construct a lasting romantic relationship, no matter how much we wanted it to happen. So we go our separate ways.

Not every breakup or severed tie comes at someone's emotional expense. It is not always an indictment on one's character or the result of transgressions. Things fall apart. It just doesn't work out sometimes. Taking the end of a relationship personally is what leads to bitterness. We make it about us being wronged somehow, which naturally gives way to resentment. We blanket ourselves inside of our victim mentality. We're angry at someone for what's been done, and we allow it to spill over into future relationships or warp our perception of love entirely.

The Four Agreements: A Practical Guide to Personal Freedom, a book by Don Miguel Ruiz is a must-read in my opinion, for every human being. The author posits how making these agreements with ourselves can lead to inner peace. One of these is to not take things personally. What people choose to do is mostly about them, not you. It's about their insecurities, values, and perceptions. Even if they do wrong by us, it's rarely actually about us. To take it personally and allow bitterness to fester is useless.

To be single, however, to be a single woman, it is often assumed that you are acrimonious about something some man did. That's why you've deprived yourself of a relationship. That's why you don't take being objectified as a compliment. You're bitter. Bitter and harsh, cold and dead inside.

The irony is that often the men who accuse us of being ice queens aren't worth our time anyway! They're jerks, womanizers, or some other type that isn't exactly what a woman would describe as Prince Charming. This is fitting because those are the ones who are typically too self-absorbed to consider that perhaps they're the problem or accept rejection gracefully.

I've actually encountered men who are bitter. This is far from a state reserved for scorn women. I've seen guys accuse partners of wrongdoing with little to no reason because some woman previously did something similar. They can't let go of the pain and anger. They're accusatory and dismissive in response to circumstances that have largely been concocted in their minds. Quick to cut women out of their lives,

I've seen men break up with partners over the pettiest grievances. They punish one woman for the sins of another.

Not many will admit this, however. Not many can see it. They feel justified in their outlook, which is often that all women are the same. They're bitter. But it's easier to designate this a female trait and slap it on to any woman who doesn't fawn over them.

There is more than one way to break a heart. It doesn't have to be in the romantic sense. I've never really known my father. Haven't seen him since I was about eight years old, give or take a couple years. I barely have any recollection of him at all. My memories of his father are a recurring visual of him stumbling around the block toward me as I played outside my maternal grandmother's house. You could tell he was handsome in his day. His hair was slicked back and he displayed a smile just as smooth. Yet, he reeked of cheap booze while struggling to remain upright and "give his grandbaby a kiss." I was terrified of him and would run screaming into the house whenever he appeared.

I said that to say I don't have the most positive images of men despite never having been treated poorly in a romantic relationship. I'm sure others can relate. From this stems the "daddy issues" attempted explanation. It's your father's fault you hate or don't trust men. It's a different type of bitterness that people will try to project on to you.

This is a real issue. Our parents offer our first intimate relationships. We learn from them how to love. They shape our perception for better or worse. If you see your father cheating and/or being abusive, it's going to influence your future relationships somehow. But it can't be automatically decided that a single woman has daddy issues or other predeterminations and hurts that have made her cynical.

I didn't have my father. His father was a horrible drunk. However, I didn't have lack either. I had another grandfather who exhibited the measure of a man. He displayed impeccable integrity while caring for his wife and family. I didn't have to witness terrible things that my absent, incapable male supposed role models may have done, largely because they were absent and incapable. I was never around for any of their potentially heinous acts.

I am intentionally magnanimous and optimistic. I believe in people, not just men, but including men, until they show me reasons I shouldn't. I've seen the shameful, hurtful things that both sexes do to those they claim to love. That idea of love simply doesn't coincide with mine. I have no preconceived notions about men being dogs or anything of the sort. Fortunately, that hasn't been my experience.

I only have a sincere desire for any relationship that I pursue to be one that is healthy, and builds me up instead of tearing me down. I absolutely want to be with a partner who is genuine, honest, thoughtful, and secure in himself. I believe that my selectiveness has been a significant factor in getting this far without having dealt with the opposite. So, maybe, the single woman is not bitter, just cautious. Not because she's been hurt, but because she's as close to whole as she's ever been and would like to remain that way if it's at all within her realm of influence.

Single.

THAT DOES NOT MEAN CRAZY

You drive men away. This is yet another unfounded assumption that many will still make when attempting to determine why you are single. They insinuate that you do things like go through your significant other's cell phone, sniff your man for traces of perfume, refuse him access to his female friends, make baseless accusations about cheating, show up at his job, curse out and embarrass him when in public, intentionally start arguments, slash tires when upset, and do all kinds of other things that one would deem crazy.

Ordinary, molehill actions and responses can be blown up to mountains that signal instability when this is assumed about you. The same things that most everyone else does are somehow different when you do them. If you scream or express anger, you're unhinged. This is because that conclusion has already been drawn. Any behavior that even remotely fits the notion can and will be used against you. You're not allowed to have human moments of exasperation.

This one is hilarious when presented to me as a thought on why I'm single. Anyone who knows me at all would list calm and collected as two of my defining characteristics. I believe that adults can disagree and discuss issues without yelling at and belittling one another. I assess situations much more frequently from my head than my heart.

If I feel like I need to go through someone's phone or otherwise catch him cheating, the relationship is already lost, in my opinion. I trust those who have shown themselves trustworthy until they give me cause not to. But long before I get to the point where I am tempted to exhibit invasive, unstable conduct, I'm going to stop and look at the situation objectively. We're going to talk open and honestly, and go from there if I still believe there is something worth saving.

I won't be anyone's fool, however. I take heed of actions no matter the words that have been spoken. What's done in the dark eventually comes to light. When that happens, I won't bust the windows out of his car, confront the potential or even proven "other woman." I will leave. Expeditiously. And I will not come back. I protect my energy and peace of mind above all else. To me, nothing is more important. You're not about to push me to the brink of insanity with constant tomfoolery.

Speaking of, often the "crazy" label is applied to women after they've reacted to actions taken by the labeler. We're toyed with, disrespected, lied to, and taken advantage of. We try our best to take it with grace, offering forgiveness and understanding. Then, when we have been stretched past our limit, can take no more, and reach our breaking point, we're crazy. As though our response was unprovoked; the actual offender in the situation suddenly becomes the accuser. He absolves himself of accountability, opting instead for the oversimplified copout of you having gone mad.

I think we may have attached a stigma to healthy relationships, equating them with boring. We all say that we want someone honest, someone true. When asked what we're looking for in a potential partner, those characteristics make the universal list, along with loyal, respectful, and perhaps thoughtful. We utter all of the right things and describe people who are likely to treat us well. We may even mean it. However, our dating and relationship choices say otherwise.

Maybe individuals with the healthy traits aren't easy to find, so we settle. Perhaps we allow ourselves to be swayed by emotion and ignore red flags. Sometimes people start out as one person and become someone else. We don't always know what we're getting ourselves into. What can be said for those times that we do?

Since forever, thrill and passion have been equated with romantic fulfillment. It's why the idea of good girls liking bad boys exists and vice versa. The good girls and the fun girls aren't usually considered one and the same. We express a desire for the ingredients of a happy, healthy relationship and true love. Yet, when presented with options that clearly contradict that narrative we choose them anyway. The excitement and the aura of mystery win us over.

I went through the usual getting to know you questions and answers with someone I'd met for the first time. When we got to what we look for in a mate or why we're single, I referenced a defiant stance against playing games and the absence of trust. I told him that a relationship filled with lying, cheating speculations, incessant arguing, and overall evasiveness doesn't appeal to me. His response verbatim was: "That stuff is fun though." Mine: *Blank Stare*

Call me crazy, but nothing about being driven mad by uncertainty, neglect, and betrayal sounds enjoyable. I don't get it. Yet, I'm realizing that to many, a calm, stable, predictable relationship where you know what to expect from the other person feels dull. There's not enough action. Apparently, we need a monkey wrench thrown in from time to time and some level of toxicity to help keep things enticing.

I understand the spontaneity aspect. Routine can get monotonous. But surprise me with flowers at work, not by disappearing for a night. Secretly book us a weekend getaway. Send me a random dirty text. There are so many unexpected conversations we can have and ways to offer variety that don't involve the erosion of someone's mental health.

That's what's happening when a person is forced to endure situations that make them feel consistently inadequate, befuddled, or unloved. That's enough to make anyone feel as though they're going crazy. It messes with your mind.

For those in search of a bond with staying power, where support and reverence reign supreme, the focus should probably be placed on characteristics like emotional maturity, discipline, and reliability. There is a bit of a trade-off here. Healthy relationships may actually be kind of boring, depending on how we measure excitement. That's not necessarily a bad thing. Boring is drama-free, steadfast, and consistent. Boring is a solid foundation on which to build.

An important job of both parties is to make the other feel secure in the relationship. You can't lie, flirt, and be secretive and then wonder why your partner doesn't trust you or starts to question your behavior. I wouldn't care at all about my significant other having the passcode to my cell phone because I have nothing to hide. Be transparent. Then, if being treated as though you are not trustworthy, you have a case for it being unwarranted. But don't walk like a duck, talk like a duck, then get upset or offended when someone calls you a duck.

Of course there are women who demonstrate erratic behavior in a relationship. Just as there are men who do the same. Being mistreated in the past, especially multiple times can make it difficult to fully trust again. Then, if and when our suspicions are proven correct, all of that previous hurt can come flooding back and cause us to react emotionally.

That is why it is important to ensure that we give proper attention to our healing. Jumping from relationship to relationship allows no space or time for this to happen. As a result, we simply partner with the next person carrying one more bag than we had with us the last time. Being single for a little while actually helps you *not* be crazy!

It allows you to be alone with yourself and your thoughts. Being single forces you to learn who you are independent of anyone else. You're able to assess your heartache and whatever has happened in previous relationships without involving a current partner. Being single affords you the opportunity to lay your burdens down instead of piling them onto someone undeserving.

When we have unresolved issues we're more prone to lashing out at an uninvolved party. That rage can only stay bottled up inside for so long before we explode. Then it's just a matter of who will be the unlucky soul who finds himself in our line of fire.

114 | Acamea Deadwiler

Be single. Get whole. Get free.

Aside from this, some just subconsciously confuse drama with passion. They feel that without some level of volatility, there is no love. I always tell people, if that's your perspective, if roller coaster interactions and not knowing what to expect from someone excites you, I'm not the one for you. I understand we all have bad days and less than proud moments, but consistency is everything to me.

I'm not for everybody. Everybody is not for me. As awesome as you are, you are not for everybody. We have to come to terms with this. Don't allow your ego to pull you out of character to please someone. Certainly don't allow anyone to convince you that your intuition is insecurity.

Single.

THAT DOES NOT MEAN
HARD TO LOVE

Not everyone will get the notion of being an adult woman who is single partially by choice. They'll think that you must be complicated and not easy to grow intimate with and that's why you have been desired but never loved all the way through.

They label you too independent. Frigid and uninviting.

Often, we try to accommodate. I know I have. We think if we make ourselves easier and more submissive, maybe we won't be viewed this way. Yet, somehow it backfires, doesn't it? Then they don't respect you. They get full of themselves and behave as though their presence is a favor. Your being overly agreeable actually becomes a turnoff. Not much messes with your self-esteem more than wondering why another person won't love you despite your trying to do everything right.

This misconception is actually more likely to come from us than someone else. We ask ourselves, am I hard to love? Or consider the idea that maybe, despite all of our amazingness, we are missing that thing that helps connect another's soul to our own. I'll answer the question for you right now. No. You are not hard to love. I can say that without even knowing you because there is no such thing.

Love is something that comes effortlessly and often inexplicably. We don't really have to *try* to love anyone. Thus, it cannot be hard to love someone. There are only different ways that we need to be loved. This is why I am a proponent of studying other people's love languages. That is a crucial element. If people take the time to do this, they will love you effectively and with ease.

We can love people with our hearts, our minds, and all that is within us—and still not love them with our actions. Not in a manner that is received by them as love, at least. We can exhaust ourselves with grand gestures and bold proclamations all we want. Our efforts will remain futile if they are not communicated in the manner that resonates best with the object of our affection.

This can sometimes lead to resentment. Often, in situations where someone feels like much has been done to show another person love and it has gone unrecognized, it's because those acts aren't translating as intended. The person on the receiving end can be appreciative of it all and still not attach any meaning. For instance, sex for some is directly correlated with love and adoration while others view it as a purely physical act.

There's loving someone, and then there is loving someone effectively. The latter is an impossible task if we don't understand how a person needs to be loved. Doesn't matter how beautiful the letter if it's written in Japanese and the person it's given to is an English speaker. It holds no more value than if it were a blank piece of paper. This goes for all types of love, friendly, romantic, familial, and otherwise.

The problem is we don't always take the time to learn one another. We love people the way that we want to love them or according to what we believe is love. We do for them things that we'd like done for us, and then are confused, frustrated, and even offended on occasion when our actions don't render the desired results. This can lead to us labeling others ungrateful or difficult when not offered the response we feel we've earned.

There is no shame in this. It's natural to communicate in our own love language. That's the only way we know until someone shows us different. We just have to be able to accept that despite our best intentions, we may not be going about things in the most effective method. We have to be open to shattering our idea of how love is shown in favor of another's.

Ego rejects being guided and told by people the way that they need to be loved. Ego takes it personally, as a slight or being viewed as not good enough for them. In actuality, we should be thankful when partners we truly love try to show us how to love them. It indicates that they care. We mean so much to them that they want us to love them well, rather than explore having their needs met elsewhere. It shows that they want the relationship to work. As does our laying the ego aside in order to invest the time and sincere effort necessary to learn.

This concept comes from the book I referenced earlier, *The 5 Love Languages: The Secret to Love That Lasts* by Gary Chapman. The book is geared toward married couples but offers tangible insight for any reader because you don't have to be married to someone to desire to love him or her or be loved effectively. Chapman goes through specific, varying displays that resonate with us as love. None of them are better, worse, or harder than the other, just distinctive.

The five love languages in his book are:

1. Words of Affirmation
2. Physical Touch
3. Acts of Service
4. Receiving Gifts
5. Quality Time

Each represents what a person needs to receive in order to feel loved. We may enjoy all of these things but don't attach deeper meaning to every gesture. If we aren't getting the one that does carry the most weight for us, we often won't feel loved at all, even if the other indicators are present.

There are other ways to learn a partner's love language and demonstrate yours besides reading the book and taking the included test. We can simply ask. Or just pay attention. Observe and listen with intent. Do we light up more when someone brings home gifts or when our favorite food is cooked? If we watch carefully enough, people tell us everything we need to know.

It won't always be easy. For example, a person who is uncomfortable with affection may find it a bit of a challenge to communicate love to someone whose language is physical touch. But if the relationship means enough to us, at least we'll know, and can learn. This way, we aren't wasting our time filling someone's glass with wine when they'd rather have water.

The truth is what's second nature to many may actually come with struggle for a few. Though I do not believe that anyone is innately difficult to love, some of us do, in fact, experience love more easily and frequently than others. I'm one of the others. If you are as well, hi. I see you. I feel you.

I sometimes have a bit of intrigued envy for the ability of others to effortlessly fall in love over and over again. I have friends who find themselves in love with every single person they seriously date. Every partner they have becomes a blissful romantic affair, even if short-lived. And if it is short-lived, they just start the process all over again with the next person—back in love before you know it.

It's never been that easy for me. In my life, instances of romantic love are far and few between. I can date a person for months, enjoy him, develop a connection but still not feel *in love*. I can have a boyfriend with whom I never envision going past this phase. It's wild, and at times frightening. What scares me is the idea that I may be emotionally unavailable against my own will.

But I've mentioned that I love . . . love. I relish the tenderness, the adoration, and passionate affection. I enjoy the butterflies and appreciate the progression of growing more and more fond of another human being. Nothing feels more magical. I look back on those rare, memorable occasions where I have encountered such a richness of relationship with profound gratitude. I am thankful for having loved and been loved because I believe it to be nothing short of a privilege to both give and receive.

This leads me to wonder, if we all want it the same, why does love seem to flow to some much more fluidly than others? For the latter, it can feel as though your test is full of essay questions when everyone else is breezing through multiple-choice responses.

Over time and through observation, I've come up with a few viable explanations:

Varying Definitions of Love

Love for me may not be love for you and vice versa. Love is a personal experience, and therefore defined personally. My idea of love involves more choosing than falling. Some may view love as being with someone every possible waking moment of the day; while others are drawn by the space to be individuals without fading chemistry and intensity.

Everyone has different needs. You could meet the exact same people, have the exact same experiences as a person in love, and it still not evolve into that for you. Some definitions may also be more common and thus come attached with needs more readily fulfilled.

Value of Companionship

Some are willing to put up with and do more than others in order to attain or maintain companionship. It's simply higher on their list of priorities.

Research has shown that relationships and romantic love are basics of our biological nature. Yet, that need will never undermine my need to be respected, appreciated, and supported. To me, these are essential components of love that are just as, if not more critical than companionship.

I also enjoy my own company and have no issues with doing things alone. While I take pleasure in having someone to join me for movies, engage in conversation, or lay around the house with all day, its weight is not substantial enough on my list of concerns to serve as a motivator.

We Find What We're Looking For

I'm a "wait-and-see" person. Those who fall in love quickly and frequently often go into the situation *looking* for love. They want it to be love before even getting to know who the person is, sometimes to the point of making it so. They aren't concerned with potentially fatal flaws or reasons not to pursue the union.

Or, they're just more open to love. Engaging cautiously can breed skepticism and keep you a bit closed off, especially in the beginning. The vulnerability that serial lovers instantly exhibit is inviting and likely comforting as the other involved party doesn't have to fret over trying to figure someone out.

It's Not Love

I believe love is unquantifiable. There is no set explanation. No rules. There is no right or wrong way to love, only the way best suited to each individual. However, sometimes what we are witnessing is not actually love; not in its pure, authentic, all-encompassing nature. Sometimes, it's codependency and attachment, masquerading as love.

Think about that next time you've allowed someone, including yourself, to make you feel as though there is some part of you that is unlovable. Consider, before you set out to fix this part, that there are many reasons why we may not fall in love as often and easily as we'd like. Seldom do these reasons have anything to do with a repelling aspect of our personality or biological design. Someone loves even the vilest human beings to ever exist. So that can't be the case.

There's a poem written by the phenomenal Warsan Shire that is ironically (or not) titled, "For women who are 'difficult' to love." It sums this idea up beautifully, painfully, transparently, and absolutely perfectly. In the poem, Shire asks the woman reading (you), already knowing the answer, if you've tried to change. She goes on to run down a list of characteristics that we've likely worked to alter in order to keep our men: closed our mouths more, made ourselves softer and prettier, became less volatile and awake. Yet, none of it was ever enough. We still felt him slipping away. She ends the poem with direct instruction, stating that if he wants to leave, we are to let him. Her reason being that the woman is a kaleidoscope of anomalous attributes, and not everyone understands how to love someone so multifaceted.

Any man who makes you feel like you are hard to love isn't the person who should be loving you. He doesn't know how. It does not mean you're complicated. To him you are an enigma, a puzzle, and he can't figure out how to arrange the pieces. Or maybe, he doesn't care to learn. Either way, rather than confront the possible ineptitude, come to you and say, "teach me how to love you," he concludes that loving you is hard.

If only we'd stop to really dig in and comprehend how a person needs to be loved, we'd discover that the process isn't more cumbersome, just different. Instead of coloring the picture blue, you make it yellow. The method may not be familiar, but that doesn't mean it won't work just the same.

It is possible that you have just been with people who didn't know how to love you. Maybe they thought they were trying to love you and felt inadequate when the arrows they shot could never seem to penetrate your heart. So they gave up. Perhaps you didn't even know how you needed to be loved.

Perhaps the issue is not the intensity of our love or our capacity to receive, but the people with whom we've been attempting to make such a sacred exchange.

Single.

THAT DOES NOT MEAN BROKEN

At a certain age, small minds will look at you and wonder why you're not married. I won't say "small minds" as a blanket statement. Sometimes people really think you're astounding and cannot fathom how you've remained single for so long. They feel that if they had the chance, they wouldn't let you get away like the foolish partners who have come and gone before them. In this instance the curiosity is a compliment and testament to the incredible woman you are.

If you notice, most of these common misconceptions stem from the idea that there is something wrong with you, with me, with single women. The small minds are those who believe there has to be an insurmountable defect if no one has yet chosen you as his wife. I always say it's not merely about who chooses me, but also who I choose. There has to be a mutual choosing. There is great disappointment on the horizon if we don't exercise this power. Consciously decide who and what you want in your life instead of just making it work with whoever chooses you.

Our bodies exhibit scientifically-proven physical reactions to the feeling of love, such as flushed cheeks, a racing heartbeat, and sweaty palms. There are chemical responses happening within us that signify love may be in the air, including the release of dopamine, norepinephrine (otherwise known as adrenalin) and serotonin—the chemical that when low can lead to depression. Research shows that love gives us a sense of happiness! And excitement. It is the ultimate feel-good drug.

Because of these reactions, we believe that who we select as a partner is at the mercy of our subconscious biochemistry. We can't tell our love chemicals not to produce or our hands not to get clammy. We can't keep those butterflies from somehow finding their way into our bellies. We fall in love. Even when we aren't looking for it and would rather not. There is a consensus that the feeling of love is beyond our realm of influence.

We may not be able to control the physiological reactions that we experience as it relates to another person. But can we choose whether or not to proceed in loving that person? Better yet, *should* we choose?

"Falling" indicates a loss of control. And while it is important to relinquish some of our reign in a relationship, plummeting into an abyss of sensory overload can be problematic. Falling in love is an emotional experience. Emotions are volatile and, more importantly, fleeting. To be led by them is to follow an impulsive guide that may or may not keep us on the same path from one day to the next.

How many times have you fallen in love and then later realized that it's not actually what you want? How often have you fallen in love, and then later saw clearly every last one of the fatal relationship flaws that you initially overlooked because neurotransmitters told you to? Before we even really know a person or ourselves or what we need and want from a relationship, we've fallen.

Love does not have to be the absence of thought. We can feel emotion without allowing it to control us. There is something to be said for chemistry and connection. If it's not there, it's not there. We can't force it. But there is also something to be said for chemistry without compatibility of values, personalities, and love languages. Those things may matter even more. When the initial state of ecstasy starts to fade, that's what we're left with.

We want passion. We want to be drawn to someone by forces that appear greater than ourselves. The euphoria of being swept off of our feet and head-over-heels for someone is unmatched. It's beautiful. I relish it, too.

However, personally, at the end of the day I want to be chosen. For someone to see all of you and choose to love you, to love you on purpose; to me, says much more than the result of an incontrollable impulse followed blindly that forced us together. Choose to stay. Choose to work and grow.

We can't just pretend that science and our body's natural responses don't exist, but we can mindfully incorporate logic before we get to the emotional point of no return. This is about adding to the process, not taking away.

They say the heart wants what the heart wants. But we'd save ourselves a great deal of heartache and perhaps build more meaningful relationships if we learned to selectively indulge it.

I've literally had this said to me, "You're attractive, successful, and don't have any kids, you must be crazy." Or something has to be "wrong" with me. There's a presumed catch. Maybe I'm cold. Maybe I don't know how to love. Maybe I'm *too* liberated. Perhaps I have some entrenched childhood issues that prevent me from trusting men. All of these scenarios have been presented or pondered, if not by others then within my own thoughts, sometimes both. Except the crazy theory, of course. I've already addressed my being as levelheaded as they come.

Maybe that's it . . . I'm not reckless enough. An excitement factor is missing. I think we often correlate haste with enthusiasm. And if you don't make decisions based solely off of emotion, if you operate more deliberately, and consciously embark on experiences, you're not spontaneous enough.

If we're not careful, we find ourselves looking for possible shortcomings or attributes that may be seen as less desirable.

I've had my issues, the greatest of which may have been not really understanding how to offer and receive intimacy. We usually emulate the manner in which we've been loved. That's our only reference point for much of our early lives. We grow to either love the way that our parents loved us, or the way we saw them love one another.

I never saw my parents love each other or had an example to follow. Not because no one ever loved me, but because it wasn't an overt, out loud demonstration. I may have known it in my head but never felt it in my heart. I've spent the better part of my adult life trying to teach myself how to effectively embrace and express this emotion.

I spoke on how I haven't seen my father since I was a small child. Before then, he'd bother with me on occasion; take me to get food or new shoes. I don't feel as though there was willful disregard. He had his own demons. Aside from the sentiment behind the gifts, there wasn't an ounce of tenderness shared between us. We were but strangers who hung out on occasion for whatever limited amount of time we both could stand. More than a decade later, he wrote my mother and me a letter as part of working the Twelve Steps in Alcoholics Anonymous. Finally, it all made sense.

My mom has been in my life throughout, but we've never had much of a relationship. I may have been an adult the first time we verbally traded the words, "I love you." We'd write the phrase inside birthday cards and such, but it was never spoken. It didn't carry any weight. We didn't hug or show affection at all. It got to a point where the mere thought of such interaction made me uncomfortable.

This was my picture of what love looks like. Passive and awkward. Sadly, the space reserved for my introduction to closeness and vulnerability remained unoccupied. I had to start from scratch with almost nothing to go by except what was witnessed in television shows and movies. I knew it wasn't real, but as a kid I watched, longing for someone to one day love me like that.

None of this means I'm any more broken than anyone else.

I've evolved in this area, through books, conscious openness, and having love poured into me by people I've met along my journey to this point. However, I'm still learning. I am still failing. I'm still picking myself up and trying again.

I've discovered that my most gratifying relationships are with those who are on the opposite end of the spectrum. Those who grew up in warm, affectionate (even if otherwise profoundly imperfect) households. They have love overflowing and give it all away without inhibition. These individuals challenge me to access parts of myself that need to be unearthed in order to receive and reciprocate their adoration. To be cared for with purpose is beautiful and empowering.

In being honest with you, and myself, I could be married with children by now if I so desired. If that was the epitome of what mattered to me. But I am much more invested in the quality of my unions than the quantity or timing. I'd never be in a relationship that I felt did not serve me just to say that I'm in one. Sometimes you actually do choose to be single because the current alternative is less appealing. If it's not right, it's not right. Doesn't matter if you're twenty-two or fifty-two.

With this idea presented, people will then say, so you mean to tell me you haven't dated one decent guy in all this time. My response is, of course I have. I've dated several. But a decent guy does not a formidable relationship make. Are we compatible? Do we have similar principles? Are we physically attracted to one another? Do we have chemistry? Do we communicate well? Do we each feel that the other is trustworthy? Are we both ready for a commitment? Can we each offer what the other needs from a relationship?

I consider all of these questions because I know how important the answers are and would never knowingly set myself up for catastrophe. I know the situation will never be perfect and if we're always looking for a reason not to do something, we'll find it. There just has to be more of a foundation than "he's a decent guy."

You do wonder sometimes though, during this process of looking for a place that you are not even sure exists, whether you are doing something wrong. And if you listen to the noise around you, to the detractors, you could start to believe it and attach these labels to yourself. The next thing you know, your self-esteem is at rock bottom as you've been convinced that it is in fact you, that you are damaged or worse, that you are unredeemable from this state.

This is not to ignore the fact that there are aspects of ourselves on which each of us could work. Our relationships could possibly be improved if we were, for example, more accepting, trusting, honest, or willing to make ourselves vulnerable. Perhaps we have obstacles here. Past pain and betrayal could indeed have affected us in some way. I for one feel that it is important that we all consistently work to become better versions of ourselves. However, don't let the sole basis for your self-improvement reasoning be simply that you are single.

Most of us are likely, or have been at some point, broken. None of us should feel inadequate when confronted with this feeling. Oftentimes, we're being too hard on ourselves.

When looking at someone who excels where we may fall short, we tend to envy how whole and healthy they seem to be. It shines a light on the attributes we believe we are lacking, making us feel even more inept in those areas than we already do. It may be that the individual exudes confidence or intellect. Perhaps they've achieved great success as a result. Maybe they were loved properly and have that piece of life all figured out, as we flounder through unfulfilling relationships. We want what they have and wish we'd traveled the more accommodating path. The thing is, I guarantee that seemingly perfect person is far from it. He or she probably just endure a different struggle.

In some form or fashion, we've all been damaged by people and circumstances. We may be in repair or still learning how to get there, but because humans aren't perfect and life isn't fair, it's impossible for anyone to have lived at all without ever feeling broken by something or someone. There is usually at least one aspect of our being that didn't develop quite as it should have or as fully as it could. We're all missing pieces somewhere. If you've been fortunate enough to elude this fate, kudos to you, but give it time. Wounds are inevitable and come in many forms.

Others may be further along in their journey toward healing, but no one is without flaws or fault. We're often comparing against pseudo-standards. Not that the image of the person we're using as a measuring stick is a façade, it's just an incomplete picture.

We're all out here trying to offer life the best version of ourselves that we have at the moment. We play to our strengths and aim to avoid situations where those characteristics that we're uncomfortable displaying may be exposed. What people show us is likely only a fraction of who they are. What we're doing isn't apples-to-apples or insecurities versus insecurities. We're evaluating what we consider to be our worst against their best. Our self-image doesn't stand a chance in this fight.

"Comparison is the thief of joy" anyway, or at least Teddy Roosevelt thought so. Some beg to differ.

They believe that it *can* be a joy-stealer, but it doesn't have to be. It can actually motivate us to improve and work harder toward achieving a goal. It's when our comparisons are unrealistic or imbalanced that doing so leaves us feeling as though we are not enough.

If we judge our social lives against Kim Kardashian's, of course, we're going to think ours sucks; we have no friends and no one likes us. She made a career of being on the proverbial scene. Maybe not on this scale, but these are the kind of impractical assessments that steal our joy. Not to mention that I'm sure even she fights other internal battles. We all do.

I hope that no one takes offense to the idea of being broken. It's not a slight. We can be defensive about it, taking it to suggest that there is something wrong with us. However, I view it more as the room that we have to grow.

Sometimes devastation is the start of a beautiful process. Being broken is not a state of which to be ashamed, nor is it a unique endeavor. This is a significant and prevalent phase of the human experience. One out of which we are completely capable of emerging from more evolved than we would have been without having withstood the lessons and embracing our scars. The benefit is that we can put the pieces back together however we like. We can arrange them differently, stronger, and with a more solid foundation. We can put ourselves back together in a manner that better prepares us to survive the situation that may have broken us down, should we be unfortunate enough to face it again.

On our worst days, we feel ruined beyond repair. We attach all of these lost-cause labels to who we are: unlovable, unworthy, heartless, unlucky, pathetic, and categorically unhappy. We water the negative seeds that have been planted inside of us. Then we fertilize them by supposing that others don't face these same or similar challenges.

We make ourselves an island, as though we're not only suffering but isolated on this course. This leads to more agony. Some of us absolutely face tougher tests than others. Yet, whether it's obvious or not, we're all in emotional distress at times. We're all just trying to figure out things as we go.

There is no one way or best way to be and heal. We could mimic exactly what someone else has done and not find the same relief. There is only the method that works best for us. Though, I do believe understanding that we are not alone—that others have been where we are and made it to the other side—is an advantageous perspective to maintain no matter our approach.

It seems that the single woman is often viewed as an unusual, more severe kind of broken. Many different variables come into play when embarking on a romantic relationship, too many to attribute being single to only personal deficiency. Timing, standards, and mutual desire are just a few.

You *should* be picky about who you entertain. You should be deliberate in your choices. This is your life, and such decisions can often result in lifetime commitments, as well as life-altering consequences. Approaching our relationships, the idea of marriage, and the like with seriousness is not a flaw. Possessing the ability to maintain a positive attitude in your waiting (or not) does not mean that there has to be something wrong with you. You can be whole and complete even if you are alone. No matter what anyone says. Single, at any age, is not and never will be synonymous with broken.

I am aware that despite all that I have expressed, some will still choose to label me, or rather us as bitter, broken, unrealistic, lonely, hard to love, desperate, crazy, jealous, high maintenance, and sexually frustrated. They'll do this despite the fact that there is no justifiable reason here to do such a thing. They'll do it because truth doesn't matter and the process of thought, for them, is too much work when the topic is not of much intrigue compared to the stories they've told themselves. Believing what they want to believe sits better with their delusions of grandeur. In making assumptions rather than facing the idea that there are other, less disparaging reasons a woman may be single or uninterested, these individuals protect their own self-image.

If one side is perhaps more broken than the other, it doesn't sound as though it's the side of the single woman.

Single.

ACKNOWLEDGMENTS

I am deeply appreciative of my friends, without whom I am certain I would not be the woman of which I am proud today. Your support, encouragement, and voicing of opinions that differ from mine have challenged me in every way imaginable. You've made me think about things I may not have otherwise, from perspectives I would not be able to consider. Thank you for giving me endless stories to tell.

Thank you to every guy I've ever dated who took the time to get to know me, instead of defaulting to the application of the unflattering labels that I mentioned in this book. You're so undervalued in this world. I hope you find, or have found what you deserve from love.

Thank you to every woman who has ever reminded me that I was enough.

To my family, who does their best to allow me to live in peace, knowing that such a state is vital to my soul—we've come a long way. I'm thankful that we've made it this far. I wouldn't trade any of you or change anything that we've been through.

There's this saying from Paulo Coelho about how when you want something, all the universe conspires in helping you achieve it. I knew that this book was special and one that I was meant to publish when I began encountering people who could help me make it the best that it could be, and went above and beyond to do so. Thank you to my Manuscript Evaluator Lyric Dodson, and my Editor Nancy Schenck.

Acamea

ACAMEA DEADWILER is an accomplished writer and journalist who has appeared on the FOX television network talk show, MORE. Formerly designated a Top 100 Contributor on Yahoo! with more than one million page views, Acamea's work has been featured on many prominent media platforms. She has held Top Writer status in both love and feminism for Medium. Acamea is also an event speaker who currently resides in Nevada. You can follow her at @acameald on Facebook, Instagram, and Twitter, or visit acameadeadwiler.com.

Made in the USA
Lexington, KY
25 October 2019